PERU'S ~~INEXPLICABLE~~ *yet unexplained* STONE FOREST

Markawasi

Kathy Doore
Forward by Peter E. Schneider

This Book is Dedicated to the tireless effort and keen imagination of Daniel Ruzo, whose scholarly insights and futuristic visions infused innovative new thought, spurred debate, and drew thousands of visitors to the high Andean mesa, to discover for themselves the mystical allure of the ancient Stone Forest, Markawasi.

"Everything is a mystery at Markawasi. After eighty centuries of abandonment, we are not able to integrate ourselves into the same vital attitude and psychology of its inhabitants. We must completely imagine this grandiose past. Only in this way will we be able to study successfully the great works of an earlier people that have arrived before us across the millenniums. These are the works of the beginnings of the Great Cultures to express themselves as a whole; to perpetuate a collective yearning. They wanted to bequeath to us an affirmation of their existence, and of their unity in a human ideal. And they did it with works that bequeathed their philosophy, science, religion and art, which, at twelve thousand feet in altitude, dominates the Pacific. These works will overload the souls of everyone that arrives to visit them."

Daniel Ruzo

Markawasi
Peru's Inexplicable Stone Forest

Kathy Doore
Forward by Peter E. Schneider

Composed in the United States of America
Printed in China

Book Design © 2006 Kathy Doore
Layout by Pat Alles
Edited by Rea Day Baker

Publisher Kathleen Doore
Surprise, Arizona

Markawasi.com
info@markawasi.com

ISBN-13: 978-0-9791713-5-2
ISBN-10: 0-9791713-5-0

Library of Congress Control Number: 2007900048

Forward

Soon after arriving in Peru 23 years ago, I heard about a strange, mystical place in the Andes Mountains, where there were hundreds of stone statues. It was said that Markawasi was ancient, beyond living memory, existing before the Incas, and the pre-Incas. It was related that there were heads and faces of human beings of different races, both male and female, and animal figures unknown on this continent. There were stories of dinosaurs and strange inscriptions carved into the rock; all this on a plateau located 4,000 meters above sea level, less than 80 km from the city of Lima.

There was only one problem: nobody knew how to get there. Finally, after nearly six months of searching, I found a group of students who were willing to guide me to the plateau, and thus began the biggest adventure of my life! It was not an easy journey. First, one had to ride on a rickety old bus, finally arriving to a tiny village high in the mountains. Here, there were only cheese and potatoes to buy, and only three horses in the whole village, with a few donkeys scattered around. There was no water on the plateau; no hotel, no food, no toilets, no nothing. However, when I finally reached Markawasi, my jaw dropped. My first thought was, "This is one of the Seven Wonders of the Ancient World, and it's right at the top of the list!"

Daniel Ruzo, the Peruvian scholar and explorer, discovered the immense carved statues on the Markawasi plateau in 1952, after having seen a photo of what the locals called, "Peca Gasha," a towering carved monument found on an obscure plateau in the district of Huarochiri. The site had been briefly referenced in 1923 by the Peruvian archaeologist, Julio C. Tello, who termed it, "Markawasi," giving a brief description of the 13th century ruins, without pointing out, however, the massive sculpted statues. Ruzo spent nine summers investigating the sculptures, maintaining that they dated before the oldest pyramids of Egypt; pre-dating, in fact, the Great Flood of Noah. He labeled it a "proto-historical" site, which he claims existed "anterior to the Sumerians and to all three-dimensional sculptures that fill the European museums!"

The figures at Markawasi are uniquely arranged over a tabletop mesa, 4-1/2 km in length, and one km wide. A three-day trek is the minimum required time to visit all the statues; a week would allow a more thorough visit. The figures tend to be found in clusters; a half- dozen can be seen in one area, and a few hundred yards further on, there are more. On the surrounding mountains, there are no figures at all. Once, while investigating the monuments, I noticed that when I walked the same route twice, I would see faces and figures

that were not there before. This effect is produced by the progression of the sun, creating a constant flow of shadow and light. When I would traverse back along the return path I'd invariably see new and different shapes. Of course, a good guide is invaluable, and I am pleased to tell you that there are a number of excellent guides available for hire in the village of San Pedro de Casta, located at the base of Markawasi. Here is where you can find provisions and a place to stay the night, which is a necessity in order to acclimate to the increasing altitude before departing for the Stone Forest, at an even higher elevation. It is nearly impossible (and not recommended) to visit the plateau and return in the same day; a multi-day camping trip is outlined in this guide.

No one is quite sure how the stone figures got there, how old they are, or who made them. Many theories abound, and some of them are presented in this book—the first definitive work carried out by a group of people whose lives have been deeply touched by the site, since the tenure of Daniel Ruzo.

In attempting to comprehend and fully understand the enigma that is Markawasi, one comes away with a lasting impression that the ancient history of this planet is quite possibly different from what our historians would like us to believe. With some certainty, I can state that the sculptors of these towering monuments were giants, immense in intellect, if not in stature (think of the faces of the four presidents at Mount Rushmore); even the stone seats are clearly made for an impressively-sized person, or two. There are various pre-Incan ruins to explore, and burial sites called, "chullpas," containing old bones and pottery shards. In addition, there are many beautiful lakes (in the rainy season), and the occasional sighting of the majestic condor.

Markawasi defies all previously-known timelines and, if not one of the oldest, it is, without doubt, one of the most curious and extraordinary of all places on the planet. It cannot be easily defined by other historical sites.

I invite you to come to Peru to discover for yourself the mysteries of Markawasi. I guarantee that you will never be the same again.

—Peter E. Schneider
Lima, Peru, April 2006

Peter E. Schneider was born in the northern English city of Bradford, and at the age of 19, he moved to Switzerland with his family. His father, Ernst, was a successful wool merchant; his mother, Edith, a naturalized English citizen. After obtaining a degree as an economist from Hohere Wirtschafts & Verwaltungsschule, Peter relocated to the tiny country of Lesotho in southern Africa, where he managed a wool company.

In his spare time, Peter researched the African witchdoctors, and also formed a band of musicians called "Uhuru," later known as "Sankomoto." During this time he developed a passion for reading all things mystical, subsequently leading to his interest in the Silva Method. He ultimately became an international instructor, teaching courses in Europe, southern Africa and South America. Peter first learned about the remarkable statues on the Markawasi plateau when he moved to Peru in 1983. He still lives in Lima, where he has developed a Rainforest Lodge, and several radio shows, including "Top Latino," "Radio Reggae," "Back in Time," and "Elixir."

It is his sincere desire that this Guidebook will kindle the excitement in others that he so passionately feels every time he visits Markawasi.

Contents

Forward 4

Preface 8

Introduction 14

Mystery of Mysteries..................... 22

A Fantastic Discovery............... 28

Expression of the Sacred Earth ... 36

The Markawasi
Stone Forest 42
  Map and Hiking Routes

Temples of Light and Shadow..... 46

 48........... Monument to Humanity
 51..................... Peca Gasha
 52..................... Chessboard
 53..................... Zodiac
 54......................... Turtle
 55.................. African Lions
 56.......... Woman with Child
 58..........................Camp

59........................... Ruzo's Cabin
60.............................Condors
61.............................Elephants
62.............................. The Cave
64.................The Camels, Llama
66.............................Chullpas
68.................. Lagoon Huacrococha
70...................Path of Viracocha
72...........................Tiki Gods
73.............................Prophet
74........................ Alchemist
75.............................Druid
76.................The Pharaoh & Nefertiti
78......................... Chinese Ideogram
80......................... The Amphitheatre
81........................... Inca
82........................... The Lovers
83.................... Soxtacuri, Puma
84...................... Gate of the Gods
86......Mastodon, Bruja, Winged Sphinx
88.......................... The Dogs
89.............................Frogs
90.........................Mayorales, Shell

91 .... Dancing Maidens
92 .... Valley of the Sea Lions
93 .... Tortoise
94 .... The Inferno
95 .... Reclining Man
96 .... Condor
97 .... Fallen Horse
98 .... Egyptian Deities
99 .... Astronauts
100 .... The King
101 .... Sphinx
102 .... Cross, Cruz
104 .... Hill of Gazes
105 .... African Queen
106 .... La Fortaleza, The Fortress
108 .... Santa Maria
109 .... The Cat
110 .... Kankausho Altar

Superbatolite Circompacifique 112

Faces & Sculptures 114

Sons of the Ray 116

Fiesta del Agua 124

How to Go! 134
Festivals, village life and outfitting for the mesa

Nature's Gift 146
Medicinal Plants of the Mesa

Voices of the Mesa 149
150 .... Dream of Masma
152 .... Eagle and the Condor
154 .... Listen
156 .... Abode of the Apu
158 .... Guides
159 .... The Els
160 .... United Paths
162 .... Children of the Light
164 .... Kathy's Story

Acknowledgements 170

Contributions 172

Suggested Reading 174

Preface

We live in an age of extraordinary discoveries; man has peered into the outer reaches of space, decoded the building blocks of humanity, and become a creator himself. We have gone further, and in much less time, than all previous epochs, yet in our fervor to forge a captivating and enlightening future, we are often negligent, forgetting our past. This book is about reclaiming our lost history, and embracing the journey to tomorrow.

Known as a place existing outside of the boundaries of time, the Markawasi Stone Forest rises majestically 12,800 feet above the world on the western Andean ridge; lying at its base along the Pacific coastline is the city of Lima, Peru.

Punctuating the ancient landscape of this three-mile long, tabletop mountain, are

massive carved effigies, including curious replicas of unknown human races and long-extinct animals. Among the effigies may be found mind-boggling images of winged sphinxes, elephants, camels, and animals, which are unknown to this age and continent. With its sixteen carved faces of the Races of Man, the massive Monument to Humanity stands out as the most spectacular and prominent structure, dominating the landscape.

Who were the builders of this phenomenal site?

Scholars of ancient Andean mysteries believe the sculpted Peruvian plateau predates the Pre-ceramic Period of Peru and the great dynastic periods of Egypt, yet holds a direct link to the Isis Mysteries. How is this possible? With its mysterious and stunning monuments emulating, among other things, Egyptian deities, and with its claims of spontaneous healings, plus recorded testimony of ultra-dimensional visitors, the mysterious plateau is believed to be the remnant of a proto-historical culture previous to the Great Flood. Cocooned in oblivion for eons, and sculpted into the ancient landscape by a mysterious lost humanity, the Markawasi Stone Forest has reawakened at this pivotal moment in history.

Wizard's Work

Included in this guidebook are literary works by the late Daniel Ruzo, the noted Markawasi explorer, historian, and scholar, who investigated the Markawasi Stone Forest, and published his discovery of the origins of an unknown proto-historical culture, whose enigmatic remnant may be found on this ethereal plateau. Much of what is known today about Markawasi comes from the mind and imagination of this great intellect, who centered his investigations near the colossal monuments, he aptly coined, the "Monument to Humanity." Upon his death in 1991, Daniel Ruzo was the sole authority on the historical legacy of Markawasi.

Gazing intently for hours upon the monument, noting the date, time, and position from which the sculptures were best viewed, Ruzo discovered one of the many secrets about Markawasi: the figures are only visible from certain positions. In his last public interview at the age of 90, he described the technique in this manner: "The explanation is very difficult, because it depends completely on the light and the point of view, the place where you're located. If the point of view changes, everything changes. And when the date changes, everything changes. Then it becomes a different point of view. I made an expedition exclusively to see the sculpture that the local Indians call the 'Inca head'; it has absolutely nothing to do with the Incas!"

Daniel Ruzo meticulously researched the Markawasi plateau over the course of several years, creating copious written materials as his legacy. Excerpts of Daniel Ruzo's work are included in this guidebook, and it is

with deep appreciation and gratitude that we honor the generosity of his family, his widow Carola, son Daniel, and grandson Javier, who presents an essay about his grandfather's research.

This guidebook is simply a snapshot of a much greater accomplishment. Over the many years Daniel Ruzo spent on the plateau, he came to believe that only a small percent of the monuments had been identified. This book details the most distinctive monuments, many located by Daniel Ruzo, and others identified after his tenure by hikers and locals who frequent

the area. A pictorial gallery is included, with images from the two most popular routes: The Humanity Circuit, and the Treasure Circuit. A two-page map that identifies the most well-known monuments is furnished. In addition, portrayed are the voices of many people who have been drawn to the mesa, including the theories, legends, and personal memoirs of those touched by the unique experience of Markawasi.

Whenever a conversation arises regarding the Stone Forest, it invariably leads to Daniel Ruzo, his theories, his affiliations, his adepthood, and his very public controversy with the Peruvian "father of Archaeology", the late Julio C. Tello. Ruzo hotly disputed Tello's claim that the stone monuments were the vestiges of erosion, and that the only human hand at Markawasi was that of a small community that emerged in the 13th century, who paid homage to many gods, including Karwincho Wallallo. Researching publications authored by Tello, Ruzo surmised that the archaeologist had never personally visited the

site, nor could Ruzo find evidence for the cult of Wallallo at Markawasi.

To this day, controversy remains over the names of the various legendary gods, the origins of ceremonial practices handed down to the current populace, and whether or not the small houses and "chullpas" (burial huts) on the mesa are the remnants of that culture, or simply the remains of a temporary outpost, a garrison for the Incas. To illuminate some of these theories, the noted Peruvian archaeologist, Dr. Marino Sanchez, comments further on the urban sector, the archaeological ruins, and the legends of the "sons of the Ray."

When questioned on the subject of the origins of Markawasi, Ruzo claimed that a vastly more ancient, "proto-historical" civilization erected and sculpted the existing rock into the monuments we see today.

"...it was the prior humanity, which devoted its time for this endeavor throughout the world." Ruzo determined that, if pre-history was before written records, then proto-history existed before the Great Flood of Noah. There remains controversy over whether a prior high civilization existed at all, as claimed by scholars throughout the ages. These beliefs were often based on the writing of Plato, citing Solon, who received his knowledge from the Egyptian priests.

Recent discoveries of great antiquity shed new light on the controversy. In such places as Japan's Yonaguni Island, submerged in 30 meters of water; in sunken remains off India's Mahabalipuram seaport and the underwater "Inca Road" off the coast of Bimini; and in the shallow waters of the Bahamas, a new perspective of pre-history is emerging. In the summer of 2001, news of a sensational discovery by a group of Canadian-Russian divers reported what appeared to be pyramids, roads and buildings, 2,200 feet below the surface of Cuba's west coast, resembling structures in the Peruvian Andes. In regards to the origin of this underwater site, Robert Schoch, who generously contributed the Introduction to this guidebook, states, in his *Voyages of the Pyramid Builders* (2003, Pages 52-53), that "The problem with explaining this as the work of humans is the depth of the waters: 2,200 feet. At no time in the past 10,000

*"May the Sun remain a young man
and the Moon a young woman,
may the world not turn over,
let there be Peace."*

Inca Prayer

years has sea level been that much lower than it is today. The observed forms could be of human origin only if the land in this region subsided dramatically some time in the past."

Theories that high cultures existed prior to the Great Flood, achieved advanced technology, then perished due to natural cataclysm, are not new; the premise is that we are now in the last days of an age, or world cycle. The theories hold that earlier civilizations are responsible for the astonishing handiwork found globally at places worldwide, including the Andean sites of Markawasi, Machu Picchu, Cusco, and Tiahuanaco. These were great cultures that possessed an advanced technology, and are the creators of the megalithic works that, today, we are still unable to duplicate. Adding to these

hypotheses are the legendary accounts of giants, the Elohim, and modern eyewitness testimony of "space brothers," UFO's, and paranormal phenomena.

Synchronicity

One cool, autumn evening in October of 1981, I sat curled up in bed reading one of the inspired works on the subject. The book had presented itself several times over the course of a few weeks, and I knew I must have it. As I sat reading, I began to notice certain ideas arise within my psyche, and hurriedly scrawled notes to myself. "How marvelous," I wrote, "to travel and document this romance with the mysteries." Great written works have the unique ability to transcend the reader,

unimaginable longing, the soul responds, opening the door of wonder.

Around this same time, I began to observe signs and subtle messages that had previously gone unnoticed. I learned that this form of *soul communication* had a name: "synchronicity". Synchronicity is the art of meaningful coincidence; the deliberate act of heeding the still, quiet, voice within, and connecting oneself with a purposeful reality. It presents a tangible mystery at our very fingertips, and is the hallmark of an inner life outwardly expressed. My imagination was set on fire; in turn, events were set in motion. That night, I consciously acknowledged this emerging awareness by scrawling these words: "Signs!" and continued, ". . . they are everywhere." I had acknowledged the ancient journey of heart, and stepped consciously upon the path of discovery.

The Peruvian

esotericist, Pedro Astete, heralded his own lifelong quest into the mysteries in his visionary, "Dream of Masma". A meeting with Astete in 1924 ignited a passion within the young Daniel Ruzo that inspired him over the course of a lifetime. In 1953, thirteen years after Astete's death, and at the age of 53, Ruzo published Astete's memoir, *The Signs*, detailing the synchronistic events following his "Dream of Masma"; now, fifteen years after Ruzo's death, we offer this guidebook. The book that had been the catalyst for my own personal quest twenty-

bringing the journey to life, allowing the seeds of creativity to take root. Thus impassioned, I set upon a deeply intrinsic and illuminating quest. I understood that perseverance and courage are required to believe that what is achieved may be greater than what is released. My inner faith and a willingness to challenge failure allowed me to embrace this quest. My heels sprouted wings. My friends took to writing my addresses in pencil. I had learned that when passion, will, and desire unite with

signs!

five years ago was entitled, *The Morning of the Magicians,* by Louis Pauwels and Jacques Bergier (1960). It details a brief account of an archaeological treasure found in Peru by a little-known Peruvian scholar, Daniel Ruzo. During the l990's, when I was first introduced to the stone monuments of Markawasi, I had no recollection of ever having come across this reference, yet, without doubt, the source of the narrative inspired an odyssey that brought me intimately in touch with others who, equally affected and rooted, had set upon their own journey of discovery.

I first traveled to the Markawasi Stone Forest for the sole purpose of viewing the stone monuments, but I came away with so much more. Collectively, the voices in this guidebook are the recorded testimonies of the many lives that have been touched by the enigma of Markawasi. We have strived to tell the story through a photo pictorial, including the many theories, conjectures, debates and memoirs. We offer this guidebook as an inspiration meant to impassion others upon their quest.

There are many ways to behold this mystery. It took twenty-five years to find my way to the Mountain, and when I arrived, it changed my life. Markawasi has sparked my personal vision and adjusted my sense of perspective in a manner that is both fundamental and profound. Certainly there can be no doubt that the mesa holds a key to our collective journey–a singular journey we traverse together. The Stone Forest is one place where this journey manifests, becoming tangible and intimately alive.

The great and enduring mystery of the Mountain beckons . . . will you heed the call?

Kathy Doore
Phoenix, Arizona, April 2006

13

Introduction

Dr. Robert M. Schoch, Ph.D.

When I was first invited to visit Markawasi by Peter Schneider during the summer of 2005, I had no idea what was in store for me. "Oh, another remote geological site with some interesting stone formations," I thought to myself. "Well, after all, I have a Ph.D. in geology and geophysics, and I am rather fond of rocks, so what is the harm in looking at a few more? Besides, the Peruvian Andes are spectacular and always wonderful to visit." Little did I realize the profound and life-altering experiences that were in store for me there, and that are in store for anyone who visits Markawasi with an open mind and a willingness to be moved by the power of the place. And it was not as if I had never experienced "sacred sites" or Earth "power points" before. For instance, I have spent many years studying and experiencing firsthand the Great Sphinx and Great Pyramid, as well as numerous tombs, temples, and other holy spots in Egypt.

It is an honor and privilege to contribute to this guidebook on the Markawasi Stone Forest. Kathy Doore and Peter Schneider are instrumental in bringing the mystery and importance of Markawasi to a larger audience.

There are lessons to be learned from Markawasi that will benefit all of humankind.

"... natural adapted features in a sanctified landscape."

These words (from John Michell, *Confessions of a Radical Traditionalist*, 2005) resonated in my mind as I explored the Markawasi Plateau. I had come to this small plateau (about two miles long by a little over half a mile wide) in the Andes, towering above the town of San Pedro de Casta (50 miles northeast of Lima), at an elevation of over 12,000 feet above sea level, to view for myself the reputed ancient monumental stone sculptures. Here, some claimed, were to be found the remains of a lost culture that dates back thousands of years, if not tens of thousands of years or more. Supposedly they created monumental carvings from the white to gray diorite and granodiorite cliffs, boulders, and outcroppings on the top of the plateau – carvings of an anthropomorphic and zoomorphic nature, including peoples of many different races and animals found not just in the immediate vicinity, but from other continents as well. There was even an alleged sculpture of the Egyptian divinity Ta-urt (Thoueris), goddess of childbirth and maternity, in her typical form as an upright female hippopotamus. If these reports were true, this would indicate a pre-Columbian culture that had transoceanic ties, and just perhaps it represented a branch of the primordial global lost civilization of which many writers and philosophers have speculated over the centuries. Certainly such reports piqued my interest, especially since I have championed both the concept of a very ancient high civilization and the idea of significant global contact among cultures long ago.

Before leaving the U.S., I was warned that Markawasi is a landscape of strange, anomalous phenomena, be they encounters with extraterrestrials (many UFOs, which the Peruvians refer to as ovni/ovnis "object volant non-identifiable," have been sighted from the plateau), inhabitants of the reputed tunnels that lie beneath the Andes, or the ghosts, witches, and spirits that some believe populate the site. Visitors to the plateau have experienced altered states of inner consciousness, accompanied by telepathic and clairvoyant abilities, whether in the dream or waking state. What might await me in this preternatural setting?

Markawasi has attracted the attention of some obscure, but nonetheless influential, figures in the arcane and occult sciences over the past fifty-some years. Foremost among these are Daniel Ruzo (1900-1991) and George Hunt Williamson (1926-1986).

Born in Lima, Daniel Ruzo was trained in law, but is best known for his studies of the esoteric, occult, and protohistory as exemplified by his interpretation of the monuments of Markawasi. Ruzo amassed a large collection of works by and about Nostradamus and wrote a book on the seer that went through a number of editions. He was also a 33rd degree Mason. Most importantly relative to Markawasi, however, Ruzo became convinced as early as 1924-1925 that an incredibly ancient culture once existed in Central and South America, almost entirely destroyed by a cataclysm many thousands of years ago – a belief he based on traditions and legends passed down from pre-Spanish times. Perhaps the ancient culture was the American remnants or branch of a worldwide primordial culture, the lost civilization of primal times. It was from this long-forgotten culture, Ruzo suggested, that our present humanity inherited the roots of our own civilized ways. The few survivors of the cataclysm, which Ruzo thought might have been the same as the biblical Noachian Flood, may have hidden in underground chambers, caves, and tunnels. Ruzo searched for physical evidence of this very ancient culture, from the time immemorial he referred to as protohistory. He thought he found such evidence in gigantic stone figures found along the Peruvian coast, but they were not clear enough to be convincing, most people dismissed Ruzo's "sculptures" as simply natural erosional features. It was all rather like seeing faces and animals among the clouds.

Ruzo called the protohistorical culture and people (or beings) he sought the "Masma." The name was not original to Ruzo, but came to the Peruvian esoterist Pedro Astete (1871-1940) in a dream while he resided in Andahuaylas, Peru. In 1905 Astete dreamt of a huge, ancient subterranean hall, filled with scrolls containing the knowledge of the most ancient ones. And Astete heard a voice repeating the name "Masma." Astete studied extensively myths, legends, and esoteric symbolism, and believed that sacred and mysterious treasures were buried in some cavern or tunnel system in the Huanca region of Peru. Astete lived in Buenos Aires, Argentina, from 1911-1923, and in 1913 a Buenos Aires periodical recounted another dream by a second person that matched in many features Astete's dream of 1905. Furthermore, in 1915, Astete discovered that the name Masma has biblical connections. Genesis 25:12-16 names Masma (Mishma in some translations, and one of his brothers is Massa) as the fifth (of twelve) son of Ishmael (the son of Abraham by the Egyptian Hagar [also known as Agar]). Each of these twelve brothers was a ruler of his own tribe. Could the tribe of Masma have reached the Pacific coast of South America? Could the mysterious gold-producing land of Ophir, to which Solomon's fleet traveled to return with gold (1 Kings 9:26-28), be located in modern Peru? Certainly Peru is known for her gold, and this was one of the prime factors bringing the Spanish Conquistadors to her borders.

Ruzo came to know Astete in the 1920s, and was convinced that the Masma of the dream was real, and this was the protohistorical culture that he devoted most of his life to uncovering. Despite his penetrating analyses of myth, legend, and tradition, Ruzo made little headway uncovering physical evidence for the Masma until 1952 when he was shown a photograph of what appeared to be an enormous sculpted head. This was the Peca-Gasha, or "head of the narrow pass" (Williamson, 1959, p. 34), of Markawasi, also sometimes referred to as "The Head of the Inca," that Ruzo and others would later refer to as the "Monument to Humanity." Ruzo quickly mounted a small expedition to Markawasi that year, and was stunned to find not just the eighty-foot tall Peca-Gasha, but also numerous other gigantic sculptures

in the rocks and cliffs of the plateau. Ruzo intensively studied the Markawasi monuments from about 1953 to 1960, living on the plateau for extended periods of time. He lectured about his findings at scientific conferences in Mexico, Lima, and Paris, published scientific papers on the sculptures, and wrote a book about Markawasi. Not everyone was convinced, however, and many archaeologists continued to regard the supposed sculptures as natural landforms sculpted by erosion. In some circles the subject became known as "Ruzo's Folly."

The Peca-Gesha is actually not just one head, but two major faces melded Janus-like, with one facing each way. These faces are evidently of different races, and according to Ruzo and others, a dozen smaller faces of various races, nationalities, genders, and ages can be found on the structure, hence the name Monument to Humanity.

Ruzo later lived in Rio de Janeiro, Brazil, and then in Cuernavaca, Mexico, studying what he believed to be gigantic stone sculptures similar to those of Markawasi. He also traveled to Bolivia, France, England, Egypt, and Romania searching for, and finding, what he interpreted as very ancient and highly eroded (and thus not at all easily recognizable) megalithic sculptures of that pre-cataclysmic high culture.

George Hunt Williamson first popularized Markawasi among the English-speaking world in a chapter of his 1959 book *Road in the Sky*. Williamson based his account on a visit to the plateau in 1957, and he also had a chance to

interview Dr. Ruzo (who then lived near Lima). Williamson, an advocate of UFO contact in ancient and modern times, associated the Markawasi structures with extraterrestrials and giants of past eons. Indeed, *Road in the Sky* is a book about extraterrestrial contact with humans on Earth, from ancient to modern times, with

speculations on the future of such communion. For Williamson, Markawasi is a "Sacred Forest" in stone where the "gods" (extraterrestrials, or crosses between extraterrestrials and earthlings?) met to plan the future. In chapters following his discussion of Markawasi, Williamson discusses the famous Nazca lines of Peru which he regards as directional markers for extraterrestrial spacecraft (or as he puts it, "beacons for the 'gods' "), supposed stylized maps of the surface of Mars found on Native American pottery,

and many ancient and biblical references, legends, and reputed evidence for giants and unidentified flying objects. Williamson then shifts gears, relating a number of UFO sightings and encounters, taken from around the world, during the 1950s.

I will leave the UFO phenomena for others to judge. However, I do not doubt that the experiences some people have had are genuine at some level. I have spoken to many firsthand experients of UFOs, including possible alien abductees. Perhaps the most important issue is how such experiences are interpreted and what they mean, rather than whether or not they are "real." Many people have had absolutely genuine, in the sense used here, UFO encounters at Markawasi.

When you strip off the overlay of UFOlogy, Williamson emerges as both an extremely sensitive individual and also an influential occultist who espoused profound ideas amalgamated with trivial nonsense, exaggeration, misinterpretation, and perhaps a bit of down-right fraud, whether on the part of Williamson or his informants. Williamson relates a couple of personal experiences on the Markawasi Plateau that, based on both my own experiences and persons I had a chance to speak with firsthand (but whom prefer to remain anonymous, and I feel that is best at the moment), are not so farfetched. Excavating a mummy from a cave on the edge of Markawasi, Williamson suddenly felt a terrific pain on the right side of his head as if hit by a blow. Only after spending two and

a half days in bed with a severe headache did Williamson come to discover that the mummy he had been excavating died of a wound and fracture to the right side of the head. At various times while on the plateau Williamson heard a strange, eerie humming sound that could not be attributed to insects (there were none), the wind, or any other normal cause. Others have heard this humming too, not only at Markawasi but also at diverse ancient sacred sites. It is sometimes attributed to energy, perhaps bound up in the crystalline structure of the rocks.

So what are the structures, the monuments, the gigantic megalithic sculptures, found at Markawasi?

I interpret the monuments of Markawasi as incredible simulacra – that is, in this case, natural objects that in the mind's eye take the shapes or forms of other entities, such as human faces and animals. I believe they were recognized as such even in very remote ancient times. The weathering and erosion of the igneous rock of which the plateau is composed gives rise to rounded anthropomorphic and zoomorphic features that, with a little imagination and insight, can be seen as very convincing sculptural forms. Indeed, the longer one stays on the plateau, and the harder one looks, the more sculptures appear. Just possibly a little retouching on the part a human hand has enhanced some of the natural monuments, but given their heavily eroded condition, I could not be certain. I found examples where the sculptures seem to have been created in stages, whether or not the creative forces were natural or man-induced. Furthermore, following a Ruppert Sheldrake morphogenic (morphogenetic) field type of idea, continued viewing and interpretation of the structures may have reinforced later interpretations.

The Markawasi sculptures are point-of-view manifestations, not typical sculptures in the round. Most can only be seen from a particular angle, and in many cases under particular lighting conditions, be it in the morning or evening, on a solstice sunrise, by the light of a full moon, or under other special conditions. Believers in the sculptures feel there are special spots that have been designated as viewing locations, and to move even a few feet from some of the spots means that the sculpture is obscured or not visible at all. Certain sculptures appear to change form as one moves, or the light changes, perhaps from a face of one race to a face of another race. Such apparent

subtlety and precision in sculpting and viewing has been used to argue for the reality of the artificiality of the monuments, but likewise has been advanced as strong evidence that they are simply natural structures to which humans bring their own meaning and interpretations. In the monuments of Markawasi we have a mirror to view our own soul. Essentially the stones and cliffs of Markawasi are like a huge Rorschach test. Among the forms that various people, including Ruzo and others, have identified at Markawasi are men and women of various races and nationalities, from native South American to Semitic to African; mostly these are facial profiles, but some of the figures consist of standing forms or reclining forms. Along with people are a diverse array of animals such as horses, camels, elephants, lions, frogs, seals, turtles, sphinxes, a hippopotamus, sea lions or seals, a crocodile, lizards, and many other forms.

The indigenous Andean peoples had a

traditional concept of wakas (guacas, huacas), which can in an abstract sense refer to laws (as laws of nature) or knowledge, or could at times be personified as heroes and deities (similar, perhaps, to the Egyptian concept of neterw [also spelled neters] or divine principles) or as cult ancestors. Wakas, it was believed, could sometimes take the physical form of uniquely shaped rocks or other natural structures. This is exactly what we may behold in the simulacra of Markawasi. The perfection and abundance of the manifestations of the wakas would make this an incredibly sacred place indeed.

There is no doubt in my mind whatsoever that Markawasi is a very powerful, energy-filled, and sacred place. At one spot on the plateau is a large cross, oriented to the cardinal directions, neatly incised on the surface of a precipice overlooking one of the small valleys of the plateau. Sometimes referred to as the "healing cross," an experienced dowser invariably picks up a signal when walking over it and I witnessed firsthand various colleagues as they lay on the cross with outstretched arms and experienced the mystery of the spot. The "healing cross" may be a spot for both physical and spiritual healing on the plateau, but it is certainly not the only area of Markawasi that has sublime healing powers, which can benefit both the individual and our species.

Markawasi as a whole, I believe, represents one of the quintessential high holy spots on Earth. There are many ways to describe it: in terms of a power point or power place, a center

of power, an Earth vortex, a chakra point of the living Gaia, or a congruence of planetary leys or ley lines. No matter what words are used in an attempt to express the nature of Markawasi, they will never do it full justice. The ineffable aspect of the plateau must be experienced. At Markawasi the sacred and spiritual are manifest. Here we find sacred geometry in its highest and most potent form, expressed raw and sublime. The stone forest of Markawasi forms a natural labyrinth across the plateau on a gigantic scale. Here is a genuine maze in which you can lose yourself and find yourself again. This is a place of death and rebirth in the greatest tradition of initiation. But at Markawasi is an initiation into the secrets of the Earth and universe, an initiation rite carried out not by humans, no matter how advanced or spiritually aware, but purely by the gods themselves. Here at times I felt that the *kundalini* of the Earth, the spiritual energy not of its inhabitants but of the very planet itself, was about to burst forth. If we could only tap this energy. . . , but we do when we tune to the innate vibrations of the plateau.

Markawasi during the dry season is a place virtually guaranteed to induce and enhance psychical, paranormal, mind-altering, mystical, preternatural, consciousness-bending experiences. It is a natural laboratory for heightened sensory perception. Here is the perfect spot for geomancy, or divination using the Earth itself as the vehicle to induce visions. Here is exemplified the ancient oriental concept of *feng shui*, the proper orientation of buildings and graves (and there are many ancient buildings and graves on the Markawasi Plateau) relative to a natural landscape through which *ch'i* (which may be thought of as the life principle) winds and flows and finds balance between its female and male components (the yin and the yang respectively). It is no wonder that this is a perfect site for shamanistic gatherings and ritual invocations, whether in the guise of the traditional language of symbolism and hallucinations, or modern interpretations (such as a mecca for those bent on experiencing a UFO). The high altitude, crisp air, cold nights, clear skies, hot days, the natural "stone forest," the pre-Columbian ruins, and the sheer raw beauty, desolation, silence, and inaccessibility are mind-numbing and mind-expanding.

I am hesitant to talk about my own experiences at Markawasi, but I will say that I was not unmoved personally. I never observed any definitive UFOs, and I did not have an out-of-body experience, but I did feel strange tinges at times. Maybe it was simple vertigo from the high altitude, but one night while part of a group meditation I did observe a strange flash of light and two phantasms (dark, apparently shrouded, short figures standing a few yards behind another member of our group as we sat in a circle focusing our energies).

The plateau is shrouded in mystery at many levels. There is even disagreement as to the derivation of the name Markawasi (Marcahuasi). Daniel Ruzo states that the name is relatively recent and means "two-storied house," referring to the stone buildings (which Ruzo regards as Inca military garrisons) found on the plateau. In contrast, Lisa Rome states that *marca* in Quechua means the land belonging to a community, and *huasi* means town, so the name *Marcahausi* refers to the land for the town or entire community, and from this etymology she suggests that the plateau was a communal religious center for the surrounding area. She contends that there are no Inca remains to be found at Markawasi, dating many of the structures to the thirteenth and fourteenth centuries A.D. Others have tentatively dated some of the buildings to a good five hundred or more years earlier.

Whatever their exact age, the remains of extensive building complexes and other structures are found on the plateau. At the southern end of the plateau is the so-called Fortress (La Fortaleza) built upon a high butte overlooking the surrounding area and accessible only by a narrow steep path up the side that ends in a crawl-space entrance. Here pottery shards can still be found among the ruins. Elsewhere on the plateau are clusters of buildings that may have been residences, offices, places of learning, and perhaps an astronomical observatory. There are also numerous chulpas (chullpas), or tombs, to be found on the plateau, some neatly constructed of stone blocks (and in some cases rebuilt in modern times) and other tombs that simply utilized natural overhangs and shallow caves on the edge of the plateau. Bodies were bound and formed natural mummies, but most of the tombs have now been cleared out and any remains removed. We did come across human skulls and other bones in one of the more inaccessible regions, however.

The plateau is spotted with a number of artificial and natural lakes and reservoirs, most of which were dry during our August, 2005 visit. Artificial dams and canal systems collect water during the rainy season and carry the water down to the village and terraced fields below the plateau.

Even today the people of San Pedro de Casta partake in a ritual festival during October that celebrates the water captured on the Markawasi Plateau. According to Ruzo (1956), men opened the festival with rituals in honor of the Huari (their pre-Inca ancestors of a thousand or more years ago deified as the god Huari that was their protector; huari means giant or strong [Williamson, 1959, p. 34]), and the women and girls carry out the remainder of the ceremony over a number of days.

Virtually no ancient inscriptions are known from the plateau. There is one major petroglyph remaining at Markawasi, although Ruzo suggested that once there must have been many. Occurring on the neck of the Pecha-Gasha, it takes the form of sixteen squares arranged in a four-by-four checkerboard pattern. It is somewhat irregular; being incised on a rough rock surface, the lines are not perfectly straight, and the lines that it is made up of are formed from double rows of small black dots. According to Williamson (1959, p. 41-42), citing Astete and Ruzo, this is a very ancient and primordial symbol, from which many later symbols were derived, and incorporates, among other ideas, the ascent and harmonization of the individual, and hence humanity, with the forces of nature and the cosmos.

The cosmos are manifest at Markawasi. I went to Markawasi the skeptic, and came back convinced that it is a very special, mystical, spiritual, mind-altering place. It is an incredible site that raises many issues concerning lost civilizations, the past history of humanity, varying states of consciousness, and the nature of reality. Markawasi is a location where, more than most sites, each person brings their own notions, molds the landscape to their own thoughts, is affected in unique ways, and brings back their own perceptions. This, in my opinion, is part of the mystery and draw of the site. Markawasi is an enchanted plateau. You owe it to yourself to visit this most magical of places.

Robert M. Schoch earned his Ph.D. in geology and geophysics at Yale University (1983). He is currently a tenured faculty member at Boston University's College of General Studies where he has taught since 1984. Dr. Schoch is perhaps best known for his re-dating of the Great Sphinx in Egypt and his studies of pyramids around the world. He is the author of several books, lectures widely, and has appeared on many radio and television programs, including the Emmy-winning documentary *The Mystery of the Sphinx.*

I saw the angel in the marble
and carved until I set him free.

~Michelangelo

Mystery of Mysteries

"The concept of the 'eternal Janus' was behind the construction of this enormous sculpture. From the west, two main heads can be seen; one represents the Caucasian race, the other, the Semitic. The former faces to the south, and the latter to the north. These two heads can be seen perfectly from the west at the points indicated on the terrain. We speak not only of facial features; the skulls themselves are anthropologically different. Below the Semitic head, a Peruvian Indian is depicted. The nose of the Semitic head becomes the chuyo of the Indian, a type of hat used in the mountains since time immemorial, in which the top is pointed and the ears are covered. The nose on the Caucasian head is broken at the tip."

– Daniel Ruzo

Ancient man gazed upward to the star-filled heavens, beheld a wondrous spectacle, and created myths to explain the progressions of the "realm of the gods," and the great elements of air, earth, fire, and water, whose force could be called upon in dreams and visions, to make order of his universe. Tales of a lost remnant, whose artifacts and landmarks found carved upon the land, were first discovered in Peru in 1952, by Daniel Ruzo, who excitedly pronounced it "the most important sculptured work existing on the earth today."

Daniel Ruzo writes that, in Markawasi, everything is difficult to explain, given the great antiquity of its ruins and our ignorance of the history of a vanished people covering eighty-five centuries. Towering eighty feet above the Markawasi plateau, and consisting of fourteen anthropomorphic figures of four different races seen by day, and two more by night, the "Monument to Humanity," with its uncanny resemblance to the multi-faced god of the Latins, "Janus," guardian of the "doorways" and "master of the two ways," is unmistakable.

Reminiscent of Viracocha, the Andean "God of Duality," Janus holds the keys to the heavens and hells to which Mankind is judged. Similarly associated with the "floor of the House of the Mysteries," whose sixteen primary squares of the Chessboard are incised under the chin of the Monument to Humanity, indicative of the great struggle between the forces of light and darkness, symbolic of the conflict of the gods and man, it signifies a synthesis of opposites.

As seen from the west,

the Monument is depicted with two faces looking in opposite directions as a man (Sun) and a woman (Moon), gazing outward from the past in the guise of an "old, bearded man," and to the future as a "youth or female," signifying the past that is "no longer," and the future that is "yet to come," in the ever-present *here and now*. Like Janus, who holds the keys to the "entrance of the Mysteries," and who is the "custodian of time" opening and closing the Ages, the Monument to Humanity stands posed at the threshold of the new Millennium. The sun, with its twelve rays, represents the eclipse and the twelve constellations of the zodiac, writes Ruzo, providing evidence that the vanished people knew the symbolic system of chess, and of the zodiac, that encompasses all human knowledge.

Dawning of Aquarius

The sun traverses its eclipse, making a retrograde path upon the zodiac; thus, the air returns to be the destructive element at the end of our present age. Precessional movement is the main cause that establishes a Zodiacal Age. The great cycles governed the lives of the ancient people, who identified the annual cycles with the world of the ancestors and the supernatural,

giving rise to an entire cosmology. "The mystery accompanies the passing of humanity from one astronomical or historical cyclic period to the following one," cites Ruzo. He continues, "The zodiacal period of Pisces began fifteen years BC, and will end in the year 2137, commemorating the entrance of Aquarius." Other traditions of the Americas purport that this great cycle will culminate on the December solstice of 2012, with a direct alignment to the Galactic Center–the Great Central Sun, whose counterpart, our local sun, "is but a reflection of the One True Source." At the end of the great Solar Year, humanity will experience an immense upheaval physically, mentally, and spiritually that will bring about a profound shift from one state to another, in an ever-upward spiral toward perfection. We now stand posed at the dawn of a new World Age.

In 1923, Peruvian archaeologist, Julio C. Tello, first noted the 13th Century archaeological ruins at Markawasi, but had no knowledge of the sculpted monumental figures. The ancient stone figures remained cloaked, yet appear in plain view for "eyes that see." This is the first clue to the mystery of Markawasi. "The people," Ruzo explained, "do not see the rocks because they lack the faith in the magical world and in all the works of the people who came earlier--those who did believe and respect that magical world, and who created works of incomparable artistry."

Multi-faced "Peca Gasha," The Monument to Humanity

Lost Remnant

It would not be until the early 1950's that Markawasi would come to the attention of Daniel Ruzo, who, after nine years of exploration on the high plateau, discovered what he deemed "a lost remnant," whose underground caverns served as refuge for survivors of the great deluge, Noah's Flood. He theorized that in South America there could be found the remains of ancient cultures precisely like those in Egypt, having drawn their technology from an earlier and more "technologically-advanced civilization, whose source it could never quite emulate and which it was unable to maintain." He set forth the idea that previous civilizations were destroyed by an elimination process which caused the near extinction of the race, and those who originally built the amazing stone cities of the Andes, extensive in Peru, were groups existing long before the Incas, who were living their own highly-advanced civilization.

Ruzo believed that the four elements succeed each other in each cyclic catastrophe on earth, following an order of retrograde: air, earth, fire and water. His life's research entailed decoding the messages that have "been recorded in stone by the people who came before us," maintaining that the Sacred Mountain signaled the location of a subterranean network of caves which served as initiating chambers for chosen groups of humans, who, secluded from the outer world

in the breast of the Mountain, just as in Noah's time, would serve as sanctuary again during the next catastrophe. Like Ruzo, the French metaphysician, Rene Guenon, considered the Sacred Mountain sanctuary against the coming storm of purification "at the end of the devastating forces of the Kali-yuga." Like the Ark, the Sacred Mountain would "contain all the elements destined for the restoration of the world, which are thus the seeds of the future state."

Dome of Heaven

Zodiacal maps representing the stations of the year, emulating the great star temple above reflected in earthen-works below, are not unknown.

Along Peru's southern coastal desert can be found 37 miles of indelible imagery carved upon the desert floor. In 1939, an American Professor of History, Dr. Paul Kosok, discovered the first solstice alignment on the Nazca pampa, which he photographed by chance on the 21st of June, the winter solstice in the southern hemisphere. Unable to follow up on the discovery, he asked his young German research assistant, Maria Reiche, to continue the research. In 1946, Maria Reiche would discover many more solstice markers and begin her life's work, painstakingly researching the figures and abstract geometrical designs etched upon the desert floor, theorizing

The Nazca Lines, Peru.

Bottom Photo: Nazca, Peru, October 2002

Is this the type of *"unknown craft,"* suspended over the Nazca Lines, on a magnetic field, as Javier Cabrera theorized?

24

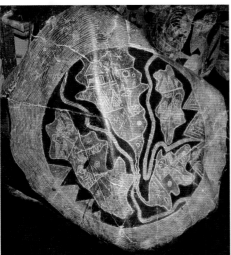

Top: Gliptolithic Man inspecting the cosmos with an optical instrument. Bottom: Hemispheres of Earth with 80% landmass, and very little water; Ica Stones, Peru.

that the earth scrapings that created the "Nazca Lines" were but an earthly reflection of a "great star temple above," whose markers denoted the cycles of time. Fifteen years later, and 120 miles north of Nazca, another mystery was unfolding, hidden in a deposit under the sands of the Ocacaje Desert.

Javier Cabrera, a medical doctor and professor of Medicine, from the town of Ica, believed the thousands of oddly-carved stones found in the Ocucaje Desert were part of an extraordinary document of human history, "a library in stone, far beyond the planetary scope and not withstanding the geological time frame assigned to the origin and evolution of humankind." Fascinated with the mystery, he spent the next 40 years collecting over 15,000 engraved stones that he termed, "gliptoliths." The collection depicts the races of man, lost continents, and the knowledge of a global catastrophe; four stones show the hemispheres of Earth at a time vastly different than it is now, with 80% landmass, and very little water. According to Cabrera, "Gliptolithic Man" attempted to manipulate the biological cycles of nature, but eventually, cataclysm resulted in tectonic shifts, massive floods, and the movement of the continents. Noting the similarity of design to the earth scrapings of Nazca, Cabrera surmised that the entire area was made up of huge iron ore deposits that concentrated magnetic energy in order to create an electromagnetic field of extraordinary strength. "A field of magnetic

deflection," he claimed, "causing this magnetic puzzle to function, forever holding the surface layer as a shadow of its former self." Among the thousands of carved stones, he was astonished to find a number of images depicting a type of craft suspended on a magnetic cushion, whose energetic field was controlled by both the surface of the planet, and the craft itself. He theorized that "magnetically-charged" locations throughout the world were understood by this highly-advanced, ancient humanity in possession of superior technical ability.

Dog of Huanca

Daniel Ruzo made it his life's work to find proof of an ancient scientific culture that left its record etched upon the landscape. In 1924, he discovered evidence to support his theory upon the Hill of Saint Christopher, in Peru's capital city of Lima, southwest of Markawasi. Located on the top of a perpendicular-angled rock, Ruzo first detected one of three carved stone heads with protruding tongues, the proto-historical "dog of the Huanca," who, like "Cerberus," guarded the entrance to the subterranean realm. "This magnificent monument," states Ruzo, "undoubtedly proto-historic, shows the great antiquity of all the human legends, which throughout many millenniums have formed a mythological occult system; they are scattered and are represented throughout the planet."

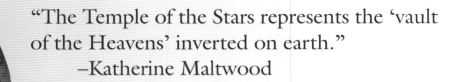

"The Temple of the Stars represents the 'vault of the Heavens' inverted on earth."
–Katherine Maltwood

Wood Carving by Katherine Maltwood; Glastonbury "Zodiacal Round Table of the Grail."

Half a world away in the chalk downs of England, another fantastic discovery was emerging. Comprised of hills, roads, and rivers, and representative of a terrestrial zodiac, a "pre-Christian celestial temple of the Stars," the "Glastonbury Giants," discovered by Katherine Maltwood, was constructed around 2700 BC, and accredited to the Phoenicians. Recent theories relating to Egypt's Dendarah Zodiac place the landscape zodiac as early as 7000 BC. Among the carved figures of the "round table" was a thirteenth figure prominently located outside the circle to the southwest – the "great dog of Langport," guardian of the sacred abode of Annwn, the subterranean realm, accessible by the dead or those still living… *if they could find the door*!

The "people of the Huanca," the "Masma," were the ancient seafaring race of Canaanites and Phoenicians who came to Peru on the ships of Solomon and Hiram, claimed Ruzo. The legends of *A Thousand and One Nights* contain many references to their travels, recounted in the story of "Sinbad the Sailor". Ruzo surmised that the Phoenicians arrived by way of the east, entering through the Amazon River and the "Rio de la Plata" (the river of silver), traveling until reaching Peru and Bolivia, the regions rich in gold and silver. Those who originated from the west, arrived on the coasts of Ecuador, and on the coasts of Peru (country of Ophir), equally in search of these riches. In Egypt, Mexico, and Peru, Ruzo found the scattered remainder of the lost race of Atlantis, for which they left their carved remnant upon the land.

During the autumn equinox of 1959, with the sun behind him, Daniel Ruzo first visited the megalithic sites of Stonehenge and Avebury, and discovered that the stones had been decorated by the same type of sculptures that had been worked on the natural rock in Peru, Mexico, Brazil, and France. Two years later, during a forty-day journey through Egypt, he proved his theory. "These cultures arise from an earlier, forgotten culture, originating from proto-historical times, in which are represented the same gods. The earlier culture suffered the convulsions of the flood, and remained witness to an 'Atlantean people', of which we have found the same traces in the Americas."

Star Temples

In the midst of Atlantis, wrote Manly P. Hall, was a Sacred Mountain, whose summit touched the heavens; sacred among many races, and symbolic of the human head, which rises out of the four elements of the body. The Sacred Mountain was the temple of the gods, recalled in the stories of Olympus and Meru. "The City of the Golden Gates—the capital of Atlantis—is the one now preserved among numerous religions as the City of the Gods, or the Holy City; the archetype of the New Jerusalem, with its streets paved with gold, and its twelve gates shining with precious stones."

Spiraling upward from the underworld to the sky, from which the canopy of heaven is hung, rises the Sacred Mountain, parting and conjoining Heaven and Earth. Here, the elixir of life flowed, and mythical heroes flourished in the realm of the immortals, who, bequeathing mankind's fate, ignited in those, "like the hero," the fervent call of their heart's desire.

Encoded in the rocky enchantment of the Peruvian Andes are the Mysteries, rooted in the Universal archetype, mirroring the supreme center of all initiatic knowledge, from where the ancient gods directed the Wheel of Time, and descended forth to judge the fate of Man.

Markawasi

"It is true without lie, certain and without doubt, that that which is below, is like unto that which is above; and that which is above, is like unto that which is below, to accomplish the miracles of the One thing." The Emerald Tablet of Hermes

A Fantastic Discovery

by Lisa Rome

These are the words of Dr. Daniel Ruzo found in the introduction of his book, *Marcahuasi: La Historia Fantastica de un Descubrimiento* (Markawasi: The Fantastic History of a Discovery) first published in the Spanish language in 1974.

"Our discoveries were made by observing rocks near where thousands of people lived; however, they didn't see them because they lacked faith in the magic world and in the works of art left by a former humanity which created and respected this world and produced these incomparable works of art, but left no signature. The artistic work was the rhythm of life, like heartbeats, or breathing, or walking on this earth. It was a work of magic. Humanity has forgotten all of this and considers going to the moon much more important. It cannot explain the appearance of these genius men who break all barriers to arrive at surprising results without seeking for himself, and without listening to dogmatic voices - which try to reduce to words that which has no name.

We demonstrate in this book that the carvings and the sculptures made in the natural rock, seen from a point of view or a certain direction, and in conditions of special lighting, give credit to a style that could only be expressed by men of profound pantheist faith. The technique of these sculptors has not been repeated in subsequent history. These works are found in different places on earth, very removed from one another, repeating the same symbols, and with one thing in common: they are found around sacred mountains, temples of lost humanity, so they won't be forgotten and that they may serve one more time to purify and save humanity."

Markawasi is a unique mountaintop, geologically unlike any of the surrounding Andes, located 80 km east of Lima, Peru. Daniel Ruzo, a genius by his own definition, dedicated his life to the study of sacred sites around the world. Upon his death he lived in Cuernavaca, Mexico, which is close to Tepotzlan, another sacred mountain site.

The works of art referred to in the introduction of his book are the monuments, monolithic sculptures, some megaliths, which are found on top of Markawasi. There are hundreds of these monuments on the 4-1/2 km by 1 km plateau. They are so large, so clear, that even someone who isn't a seeker cannot argue their existence. The "monuments repeating the same symbols" are found in Tepotzlan and

Guanajuato, Mexico; Rio de Janeiro and Vila Velha in Brazil; Lake Titicaca, San Cristobal and Los Angeles in Peru; Stonehenge and Avebury in England; The Sacred Valley of the Kings in Egypt; the Carpathian Mountains in Romania; and Kakadu National Park in Australia, to name but a few. Although Daniel Ruzo also studied the monuments of Easter Island, he made no conclusion about their origin. All of the monuments in all of these places, according to Ruzo, were created by a humanity that lived before the time of the flood for which Noah built his Ark.

The monuments mark the general area of the caves and caverns that made possible the salvation of our humanity, and those previous, during the time of the great catastrophes. The last catastrophe was a flood and Noah's Ark is merely a metaphor for the caves and caverns, marked by the monuments, all over the world. According to Ruzo the catastrophe (a fire, previous to the flood) was survived by a remnant of humanity, personified by the story of Adam and Eve, living deep inside caverns.

Daniel Ruzo formed his theory of humanity in the 1920's. It was his life's work to support his theory. Using the *Bible*, myths and

Daniel Ruzo at his home in Cuernavaca, Mexico, 1990.

29

legends from around the world, the works of Nostradamus, astrology, and other sources, he sights evidence that illuminates his belief. The theory is: Human life on earth has been made up of five humanities; each humanity lasts 8,608 years and is made up of four sun cycles of 2,125 years each. We are in the fifth humanity. Every 8,608 years the earth suffers a catastrophe. Following the zodiac, humanities have survived catastrophes of earth, fire and water. According to Ruzo, the next catastrophe will be by air and will occur between the years 2127 and 2137.

The monuments around the world mark the entrances to the caves and caverns that will make possible the salvation of the seeds of humanity. As the monuments are only indicators that these all-important entrances are in the general area, we, the faithful, must make it our mission to locate the entrances, in time to prepare the caves and caverns before the next catastrophe and save the seeds of humanity as they have been saved by the previous humanities. The universal symbols referred to in the introduction of *Markawasi* are the key to understanding how to locate the entrances on the sacred mountains. As the entrances have yet to be found, we must work to 'break the code' of the symbols to find them.

Daniel lived on Markawasi for a few months at a time over a period of nine years, during the dry seasons, beginning in 1952. He took thousands of photographs of the monuments during that time and found that, depending on the time of day, and the time of year, in the light of the sun, the moon, or the stars, even in shadow, that different sculpted images can be seen, even in the same monument. The main monument, the Monument to Humanity, has fourteen faces visible by the light of the sun, and two visible only by the light of the moon.

Ruzo's photos demonstrate very clearly the many different faces of Markawasi. He claims that even though his work went on for a lengthy nine years that he has studied a mere ten percent of the figures. Other important monuments are the Condor, whose form changes every sixty degrees, and the Cat that can be seen only during the week of the winter solstice.

Top left: Daniel Ruzo near the Monument to Humanity, 1952. Bottom: Ruzo (center) with visiting professors; July 1958.

Healing Energy Vortexes

There are many other important facets of Markawasi, all pieces of an incredible, complex puzzle. There are twenty-two energy vortexes called 'cruzes,' or crosses, made up of three distinct types of energy. There are three of the first type which are found in areas of limited access on the plateau–limited to those prepared to be near such powerful energy. The second type of cross, of which there are seven, are crosses that betoken the days of the week. There are twelve crosses of the third type, which have to do with the phases of the moon. Each cross has a specific healing power. The crosses,

which are easily visible on the plateau, have an undeniable energy that can be felt without any special preparation or sensitivity.

Carlos Seclan, a Peruvian student of Daniel Ruzo, had an extraordinary experience at one of the vortexes of Markawasi. He had been studying Markawasi for fifteen years when he had a car accident that left him paralyzed in bed for eleven months. With the finest doctors in Peru unable to treat him, he was told that he could not be healed, and would never walk again.

After having studied the energies of the

stones and vortexes of Markawasi, he knew that there had to be some way to cure his broken back with the profound forces of the mountain. He knew that on a certain day, at a certain hour, at a certain vortex, there would be the appropriate energy to heal him. He convinced his friends to carry him up the mountain to the designated vortex, where they left him alone for seven days.

On the seventh day an ordinary-looking Peruvian man, a stranger to Carlos, appeared. They spoke about Carlos' problem and then the man began to demonstrate some exercises, which Carlos followed. As he moved through the exercises he felt a heat rising through his body starting at his toes, with a distinct buzzing noise, followed by a tingling sensation which began to move throughout his body. When the heat and buzzing sensations reached his head he was aware of a light entering the top of his crown, at which point he fell asleep.

When Carlos awoke several hours later, he was surprised to realize that not only could he sit up, but stand as well. The stranger who had assisted him was gone. Carlos was able to walk down the mountain alone, unassisted, to join his friends who had been camping nearby.

To this day, Carlos is the most important living scholar of the vortexes of Markawasi. He has revealed the location of five of the vortexes. Two of the vortexes are easy to find on the plateau; one is located beneath the Cat, and the other, marked with a white X, is in the center of the plateau at the edge of a precipice. Carlos first went to Markawasi in 1973 on a hunting trip and says that before he went, he had seen Markawasi in his dreams, and when he arrived, he knew exactly where to go.

Markawasi is also a famous location for UFO sightings which the villagers call OVNI's. The villagers in the pueblo below Markawasi accept UFO sightings as a normal occurrence. When asked if they believe in UFO's, they react as though it were a strange question, as though they had been asked if they believe in cows!

Moises Bautista, former president of the community, tells of an encounter he had in August of 1963. The night was clear with a full moon. At about 2:00 a.m., he was walking near some ruins on his way to check his cows on the plateau. He saw a 'car-like' vehicle come out of the sky and land about 20 meters in front of him. He hid beneath a tomb as the encounter unfolded.

The vehicle was about three meters in diameter with six round fluorescent lights. Out of the vehicle came five beings, each approximately one meter, 20 cm tall. They were wearing orange/brown body suits and boots. They emerged from a portal of the vehicle made of clear material. They walked around and touched stones on the ground, as though they were inspecting them. They then returned to the vehicle and departed, flying north, the same direction from which they came. The whole encounter lasted

three minutes. Moises speaks freely about his encounter, as it is not considered a crazy subject in the town of San Pedro de Casta.

Others in the village who have had sightings include the town baker. He says that he regularly sees a silver metallic disc with multi-color lights flying over Markawasi. He believes that the UFO's have a regular pattern, appearing at the end of the month. The baker, and many others in San Pedro, including the town's youngest children, had a sighting at night of a disc that flew over the town. The children animatedly tell of the 'flying saucer' or 'planet' with colorful lights that flew over their heads in 1988.

Village Life

San Pedro de Casta is the folkloric Andean village through which one must pass before arriving in Markawasi. Here, one can hire burros to carry supplies and equipment to the plateau, a three and a half-hour walk up the mountain. The people of San Pedro are the spiritual guardians of the meseta of Markawasi. It is their responsibility to see that those who are welcomed to the meseta feel safe and cared for during their stay.

The people of San Pedro are 'campesinos,' or peasants. They make their communal living (income), by farming the terraced land of the surrounding mountains, as their ancestors did for thousands of years before them. A total of twenty tons of corn, alfalfa, potatoes and other crops are exported every year. More interesting, however, is that they export FORTY tons of medicinal plants which grow wild on the surrounding mountains, as well as on Markawasi itself. The few available plants found in the area seem to cover all of their needs. The people of San Pedro de Casta claim that the plants are ancient.

Stone Forest Legends

The place on the meseta with the most interesting stories is the 'Infernillo,' Inferno, or the infernal place. It is a large rock crevasse about twenty feet deep. It is said that anyone who dares to jump across the Infernillo will be 'swallowed up' and taken inside the earth, never to return again. Another myth surrounding the Infernillo is that if a person walks into the base of the crevasse, he will be taken inside the earth, go through the mountain, and come out at the mouth of a river far away. The person would never be the same again and unable to reenter society. He would shy away from humans as wild animals do. The locals do regard these as myths and readily jump over the gap of the Infernillo.

Soxtacuri was the living god who ruled over the entire plateau of Markawasi. Every January he would meet with all of the chiefs of the surrounding valleys to exchange ideas. These legendary meetings are remembered today in a ritual performed every January 5 by the 'curandero,' or shaman, of San Pedro de Casta, Paolino Gonzales, in front of the monument of the Bruja.

Every year the people who lived in Markawasi would offer a sacrifice to their beloved Soxtacuri. One year the people failed to make their offering, and in anger, he left and moved to Bolivia. It is said that when Soxtacuri left, his godless people also moved from the plateau. By the time the conquistadores arrived, new peoples populated the meseta of Markawasi. Soxtacuri's house and throne still remain on the plateau.

The conquistadores again displaced the

people of Markawasi. Some of their descendants live in San Pedro de Casta. The Spanish displaced people all over Peru and put them in new villages so that they could enforce order and force Catholicism upon them. They taught Spanish and catechism to the indigenous

There are some very attractive features on this mountain, 4000 meters high, as well. The silence is moving to the soul. At nighttime, with the stars above serving as both the ceiling and the walls of the plateau, one has the sensation of being in a large room. The views of the sea of clouds below the mountain and the islands of mountaintops peeking out are breathtaking. The not-so-occasional sight of one, two, or three condors flying overhead is unique.

There are a few forms of animal life on the plateau. The gray fox lives in a rocky den and is rarely seen. The 'viscacha', an odd cross between a rabbit and a squirrel, is the most populous animal of Markawasi. Puma or mountain lions live at altitudes higher than Markawasi, but come down to the plateau during the rainy season. All of these animals are hunted as the locals enjoy their meat as a delicacy.

In recent years the monuments and tombs have been greatly disturbed by the increasing numbers of tourists each year who make treks to the mountain. The guardians from San Pedro de Casta cannot control the destruction of the monuments, as, unfortunately, they are dependent on the income brought to the town by the visitors, who rent their burros and buy a few supplies, such as water, and firewood.

Peruvians. The conquered people living nearest Lima lost their native language: Quechua. Most names of rivers, mountains and gods are in Quechua, which, despite the efforts of the brutal conquistadores, is still the secondary language in Peru. Markawasi, in Quechua, simply means house, or town.

There are five towns in ruins on the plateau of Markawasi. It is thought that at one time, probably in the fourteenth century, thirty thousand people may have populated the towns of Markawasi. Judging from one prominent ruin, the 'Fortaleza,' or Fortress, which occupies the second highest hill of the plateau, the people were concerned with surveying and protecting their territory.

The Incas did not arrive until the majority of the towns had been abandoned and the ruins converted into 'pacarinas' dedicated to the ancestors of the departed people. What the Incas did find were constructions of angular stones put together with mud, forming patios, rooms, corridors and tombs. The tombs, or 'chullpas,' are still scattered all over the plateau, and mark the most sacred spot in every town. Unfortunately, most of the chullpas have been robbed of their mummies and offerings that included jewelry, pottery and textiles. However, an impressive display of mummies can be viewed at the Museum in the village of San Pedro de Casta. No organized excavation of any kind has ever been done in the towns of Markawasi. The Peruvian government has no funds and all excavations going on at this time in Peru are funded by foreign foundations.

The terrain of Markawasi is rocky and barren. The weather in the dry season (May through September) is hot and sunny in the daytime, and very cold at night. There is little shade from the sun. In the rainy season it is virtually impossible to walk around the plateau, as it converts into a giant mud puddle. Nonetheless, Markawasi has an indescribable magnetism that brings people back again and again.

The trip from Lima to San Pedro de Casta by car takes about four hours. There is a new hostal in town with simple rooms and showers should one wish to spend the night. It is advisable to bring camping gear, a sleeping bag, tent, and personal food supplies. The walk up to the meseta of Markawasi takes about three and one-half hours. There are a few horses available for hire that can substitute for one's own feet going up the hill. Burros for hire are somewhat small and not recommended to carry an average person. Sleeping mats and wool blankets can be rented in the village. Bring your own tent and cooking gear. The ideal time to go to Markawasi is from April to October.

The book, *Marcahuasi: La Historia Fantastica de un Descubrimiento*, by Daniel Ruzo, seeks to spiritually reunite those human beings that are convinced:

"That a humanity, so important as ours, radiated from the face of the earth because of a displacement of the waters of the planet. That the necessity to locate the sacred orchards, the sacred mountains, and the subterranean caverns where this humanity can use the telluric powers of the earth to give back equilibrium both physical and sociological. The necessity to discover and arm these caverns made possible during the cataclysm of Noah, the salvation of some chosen groups trained to realize a mission: the salvation of the human seed.

The necessity to study the seeds, the domestic animals, and the fundamental knowledge inherited from this lost humanity that is indispensable to start a new humanity. The necessity to save the myths and legends, the related symbols, the notion of 'The Treasure,' and the concepts of sacred books, the traditional revelation that we must pass on to a new humanity.

This commitment is indispensable in every humanity for the salvation of the hero, the possibility of the super man. We will reunite like this, although we may never meet all of those people who look to the future with anguish and who are seeking, in the most ancient wisdom and in the prophecies, the health and salvation of man in the physical world. This will contribute as well to the psychological preparation of the chosen. Only the union for such lofty ends can give a sense to our lives before the inevitable cyclic catastrophe."
Daniel Ruzo (1900-1991)

Lisa Rome is a journalist, chef, and author; she first visited Markawasi in the early 1990's while on assignment in Peru to interview President Alberto Fujimori for RAI2, the Italian national television network. She was the last person to interview Daniel Ruzo at his home in Cuernavaca, Mexico, before his death in 1991. She has traveled to sacred sites all over the world. Her home is in Malibu, California.

Expression of the Sacred Earth

by Javier Ruzo

Markawasi is a living symbol of an expression that conveys itself from nature. It doesn't want to divorce itself from nature; it wants to integrate with it. If you walk at night in the moonlight you will find yourself surrounded by a mystery--shapes that take you deep into your unconscious mind, to the very heart of great legends; you have entered a millennial theater. —Javier Ruzo

My grandfather, Daniel Ruzo, studied the *Bible* and other literary works pertaining to all ancient cultures, comparing their chronology, prophecy, mythology and archaeology in his search to find common ground. He derived the study of Markawasi from proto-history and myths, from legends, and how civilizations coincided in many guises. He was a man interested in solving a long-hidden mystery. His life's work was to recover the remains of lost civilizations in order to unite all the universal mythologies with a common origin. I think that this passion led him to link more information about various places, which involved him in a quest; putting together all the elements took him fifty years. In him you find more than the kind of person who came out of a university--you find a pioneer who knew what was necessary, so that the truth, the real story, was put in order. We must have pioneers who pull back the veils of history, and in his case he literally defied time.

Daniel's work on the Markawasi plateau lasted several years, beginning in 1952. His relationship with Markawasi was the most important of his studies, allowing him to formulate his theories of sacred sites, especially sacred mountains, in all parts of the world. He lived in Romania, Brazil, France and Mexico, and traveled throughout Asia and Africa, searching different sites of historical and sacred significance and relating these places to a similar method of light and stone that would create sculpture aligned with the movement of the sun, a similar ancient chronology. For example, in the area of Tepoztlan, Mexico, there is a cave with a floor full of meandering markings of labyrinthine design–a sacred symbol. The site was used for many generations, and in studying the Mountain, he found gigantic sculpted figures that ultimately beckoned him to remain in Mexico for 20 years. He traveled and lived his life in the vicinity of the sacred. The movement of light during an entire year made it necessary for him to chart long expanses of time, thus he would live in a place until his work was fully comprehended and completed.

In Markawasi, he built a cabin a few hours from his home in Chaclacayo, east of Lima, and lived there every summer. This is how he studied the places of interest; he would return to the city for supplies and to develop photos. At the age of fifty-five, he lived on top of the mesa at 12,000 feet above the sea, with difficulty and diligence, since at that time there was no road, and supplies were limited. He was impassioned. His discovery at Markawasi continued to broaden over time. It was a passion very difficult to present to the public, but he did so until his passing. The quality of a pioneer was his greatest merit. He deemed it his responsibility to preserve this legacy for future generations. Part of that legacy consists of the information regarding those World Cultures based on stone, pyramids, and societies with no written record, but that represent a vision of a different manner of understanding the cosmos and time, thousands of years before our present technology.

These ancient, sacred sites are glimpses of pre-history and proto-history that continue to mystify us to this day, and bond together the study of time and cosmos in a magical-religious

Adam Kadmon,
technica mixta, 1998,
Javier Ruzo.

sense. The ancient people were not primitives; quite the contrary, they left us a mythology that, if it is summarized, you find all the information about humanity, the complexities of astronomy and collective conscious of an ancient race. In a certain sense, I think that Markawasi, as well as Tepoztlan and other places in the world, propose symbols relating to man, his relationship to his world and the task of continuing these traditions to prepare man for new cyclical catastrophes.

To work stone with the specific purpose of utilizing light as a moving element is the highest expression of art, light being the paint brush of the artist. We see the figures come and go with light; this was the way to signal the importance of studying the movement of the planets and the sun, a chronology with which the figures are marked--a marvelous integration. Egyptians worked with this same technique, as did the Mayans, the Inca, the Tiahuanacan, the Cambodians and the megalithic cultures of the West.

As an artist, I have never found a better work of art than that found at Markawasi;

imagine carving a stone with three faces mingled together, and then adding the element of light. The same influence can be seen in the Giza pyramids in Egypt, another demonstration of chronology and alignment. It is very probable that the Egyptians had the goal of transmitting information to the future. The Mountain symbol continues in a desert; a pyramid is a mountain aligned with the cycles of time, a supreme achievement.

The ancient custom of transmitting information by way of stone and the management of sacred space, like that which occurs at Markawasi, recognized precession and the use of solstice markers to specify their rites of passage. They understood the significance of global cyclical catastrophes. This information has been passed down by way of epoch cave paintings of which we have examples, dating back 40,000 years; a continuum existing all over the world.

There is a universal tradition about the use of stones for various purposes, especially religious, designating sacred space and the exact placement of stones. This is a mystery very much related to

Markawasi. The Incas used older sites such as those of Sacsayhuaman, and Kenko, near Cusco. The principle stone in Kenko is encircled by cut stones pointing out an immense boulder that appears to be the remnant of a puma. Why would you mark a stone that has almost no form? This would be because you want to leave it as a ritual element, an offering, to the remains of prior epochs, to convey a mystery, or a truth. It was most probably a stone used long before the time of the Inca, and related to the existing sacred cave. All Inca sacred places have tunnels and ritual caves; all over the world we find the same story: the Mountain with the inner cavern; a burial place where you were "reborn" in the purifying essence of the Mother earth.

The entire area above Cusco near Sacsayhuaman is a place with labyrinthine forms, caves with entries and exits, including markings like snakes, which show the underworld as a symbol. All of this cave culture, of underground water, of the universal virgin, is also related to Markawasi in that there is a devotion to a sacred place in the two elements of the Universe: as above, so below; the virgin with her different names: Pachamama, the earth mother, the European black virgins, and various other themes, having tremendous relation with the prayers to the mountain, the prayer to Mother Earth.

Markawasi is, in the end, the natural expression of a mountain with its many special formations, as if the Earth had given birth to a full collection of mysteries in stone. When human beings behold this mystery, we are struck by the same impressions that persons living thousands of years ago had felt; therefore, Markawasi is an expression of the Sacred Earth and a message to the future era.

Markawasi cannot be understood as a

Womb of the Pachamama, Kenko; Cusco, Peru.

38

Marcahusai, Boveda Terrestre; Oleo sobre Tela, 1997. Javier Ruzo

sculpture in each stone, but as a place where all the stones, whether re-touched or natural, confer a message. Here are displayed the values of man, his knowledge of the seasons, and his often magical relation to the Universe. They used the elements of sun and shadow to work their art, where they united the affinities of sky and earth with the universal solar clock, marking where man held ceremonies to record the passage of time. In Markawasi, one sees reflections of his inner self; imagination made manifest, a mirroring of our most secret yearning.

Sacred places require one thing--that man has a relationship with them. In Peru you have the tradition of "ayni," the apu "mountain gods", or whatever you consider to be Divine. You give it your prayers, your dedication, your offerings, and it reciprocates in kind--this is ayni. All of Peru is full of sacred mountains; some have their own prayers which are thousands of years old. Today you find in the northeast Brazilian mountains cave paintings that are 30,000 years old, whose carbon dating have changed the written history of earth. This will continue to expand our knowledge until we discover the pre-existing immense cycles that rule the ages of our Planet.

History changes constantly because people are pioneers who sacrifice themselves in the quest for knowledge. I say that they sacrifice themselves because bringing new things to history requires people who devote their life to finding the hidden knowledge. From the time of Copernicus to present day, free-thinkers have been condemned or ridiculed for their pioneering spirit. There will always be an academic side that will want to maintain a stable history, but history is never stable. History is a human version of reality. It is a continuum that changes with time, transforming itself. Thus, the fundamental element for change, for any person who wishes to make real history, is to valiantly propose new theories, and this is how new elements come into play.

When I was sixteen, I went to Markawasi for the first time. My grandfather, who was more a father figure, helped me go to Europe to study art. I left my career in economics, and ended up taking photographs and traveling with him. I think that my themes have always been about the inner symbols and the voyage of discovery that one has with the universe. And the places where art took me are related to Markawasi, China, Egypt, Mexico, Europe and other places that I visited. The same themes influenced my photography and painting.

It is impossible to not join art and Markawasi. If I wanted to sculpt stone and light on a small scale today, to see how the system of cutting a stone so that the light in certain moments of the day would give form to an eye, or an eyebrow, or a nose, it is with great difficulty, because in one single stone you could have three faces, or more, like in Markawasi. Imagine one single stone, with three different figures, different profiles, some with the same nose, but one has the forehead of another's cheek, or chin; you have mixes of eight elements of the face. These combinations are not from nature. In Markawasi, one can find this art that exists in the major part of history related more to the imagination of man than to figurative precision; you find this in certain cave paintings as well.

There is a continuum in religious art since the shamanic period, so that one finds tremendous similarities with the manner in which the art was created using symbols that are universal, arriving to present time. I made this relative to my studies, finding the same symbols in all that is universal. Humanity has symbols in all cultures of the world that are similar. The circle with the dot in the middle is the first symbol of the Universe, defined with man in the middle. The cross is the fundamental element of the human being as a person with the top part as the sky, the bottom part as the earth, and in the middle is the human being. The "axis mundi," world center, is a fundamental element in all cultures. All these elements of universal symbolism are found in Markawasi, the classroom of nature where this wisdom is taught.

We think that we can understand the human being. Thus, the artistic expression for these thirty thousand years or more of ancient history is fundamental, because this was humanity's greatest expression, its unity with nature and with the symbols and movement of the universe. The movement of the sun gives us the first standard model of time. The artist is dedicated to making perennial truth, and the most universal truth is time. You can go to a pyramid in Egypt, China, or India and find all of the shapes, all of the mysteries, and all of the relationships with respect to energy, sex, and chronology; they are like books.

Our way of understanding art is either courteously polite, or very technological. However, thank God there exist people who try to bring forth the heritage of the human spirit, not only throughout the last two hundred years, or the last fifty years, or in the advertising of present times. Symbolism is everlasting. It is everywhere. The great mythologist Joseph Campbell stated it very clearly, and we feel it is true, because, in the end, one does not try to make a work of art that represents something that is so ephemeral that it is almost useless except in revealing the mysteries, but it includes making the art *come alive*. This is another subject that Markawasi has taught me. Living art gives life to a symbol. For example, in dance, a position carries energy; one form of this is Tai Chi. In Zen painting, you have a direct relationship between the mundane life and the symbols. Physical shapes are symbols that carry energy because they transform energy from

Javier Ruzo

Javier Ruzo, grandson of Daniel Ruzo, is a professional artist, photographer and painter, who studied at London's prestigious Chelsea School of Arts; in Paris, at Cité des Arts, and at New York's Pratt Institute. He completed his studies in the symbolic meaning of art at the Massachusetts College of the Arts in Boston. Since 1982 his work has been featured in contemporary museums worldwide. When not traveling, he lives and paints at his home in Lima.

the earth to the human being. Thus, all artistic endeavors can be symbols, and sacred symbols are our connection with the Divine.

In the end, Markawasi is a living symbol of an expression that conveys itself through nature. It doesn't want to divorce itself from nature; it wants to integrate with it. A mountain of stone emulating time and imbued with the knowledge of the earth, Markawasi is a book of symbols, a place of sacred knowledge. It gives something essential to the people who go there. It refreshes and transforms their imagination, making them feel like they are entering a mystical gallery. If you walk at night in the moon light, you will find yourself surrounded by a mystery--shapes that take you deep into your unconscious mind, to the very heart of great legends; you have entered a millennial theater.

I think the artists of earlier epochs wanted to transmit the perennial nature of the human race, the understanding of the universal mythology, the unrevealed treasure of Ali Baba, the treasure of the caverns. These are treasures bringing us to the same point. It is not a treasure of money, nor of gold, or silver – it is the treasure of human understanding and knowledge. The most difficult task of those who pioneered, who passed on the knowledge from hand to hand, like a jewel transmitted to the future, is the knowledge of the treasure, and its repository: the sacred mountain.

41

Markawasi Stone Forest

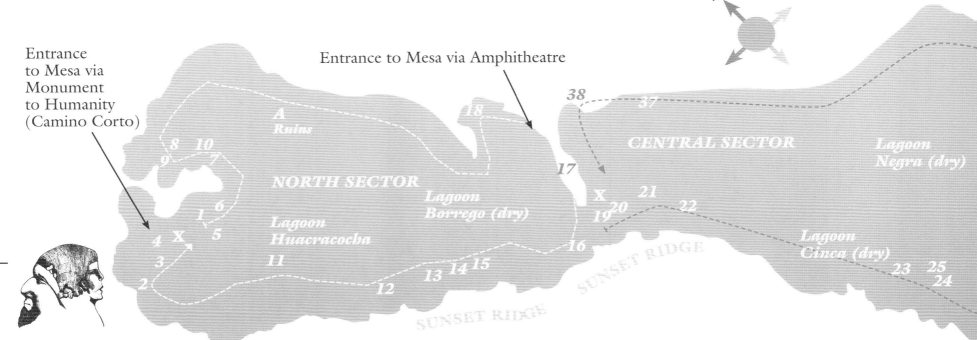

Entrance to Mesa via Monument to Humanity (Camino Corto)

Entrance to Mesa via Amphitheatre

N

A Ruins

18

38   37

CENTRAL SECTOR

Lagoon Negra (dry)

8 10

9   7

NORTH SECTOR

17

6

Lagoon Borrego (dry)

X

19 20   21

22

1

4 X

5

Lagoon Huacracocha

16

Lagoon Cinca (dry)

3

11

13 14 15

23   25
         24

2

12

SUNSET RIDGE

SUNSET RIDGE

44

HUMANITY CIRCUIT *Suggested Itinerary 1/2 Day*

Beginning at the Monument to Humanity in the North Sector and traveling clockwise to the Amphitheatre and Return:

Monument to Humanity, Woman with Child, Condors, Cave, Camels, Chullpas & Ruins, Lovers, Amphitheatre/Inca, Ideogram, Pharaoh, Alchemist, Prophet, Druid, Lagoon, Lions, Turtle, Elephant, and Ruzo's Cabin.

TREASURE CIRCUIT *Suggested Itinerary: Full Day*

Beginning at the Gate of the Gods in the Central Sector to the Fortress on the far South Sector, and return:

Gate of the Gods: Sphinx, Mastodon, Bruja, Dogs & Frogs, Mayorales (Dancing Maidens), Sea Lions, Tortoise, Inferno, Reclining Man, Fallen Horse, Healing Cross/Vortex, Hippo, Crocodile, Astronauts, Condor, King, Sphinx, Fortress: African Queen, Gazing Figures, Archaeological Ruins, Cat, Santa Maria, Ruins, Kankausho, Seat of Soxtacuri

Archaeological Ruins
A, B, C, D

April through October all lagoons are generally dry except for Huacracocha.

The Markawasi Stone Forest

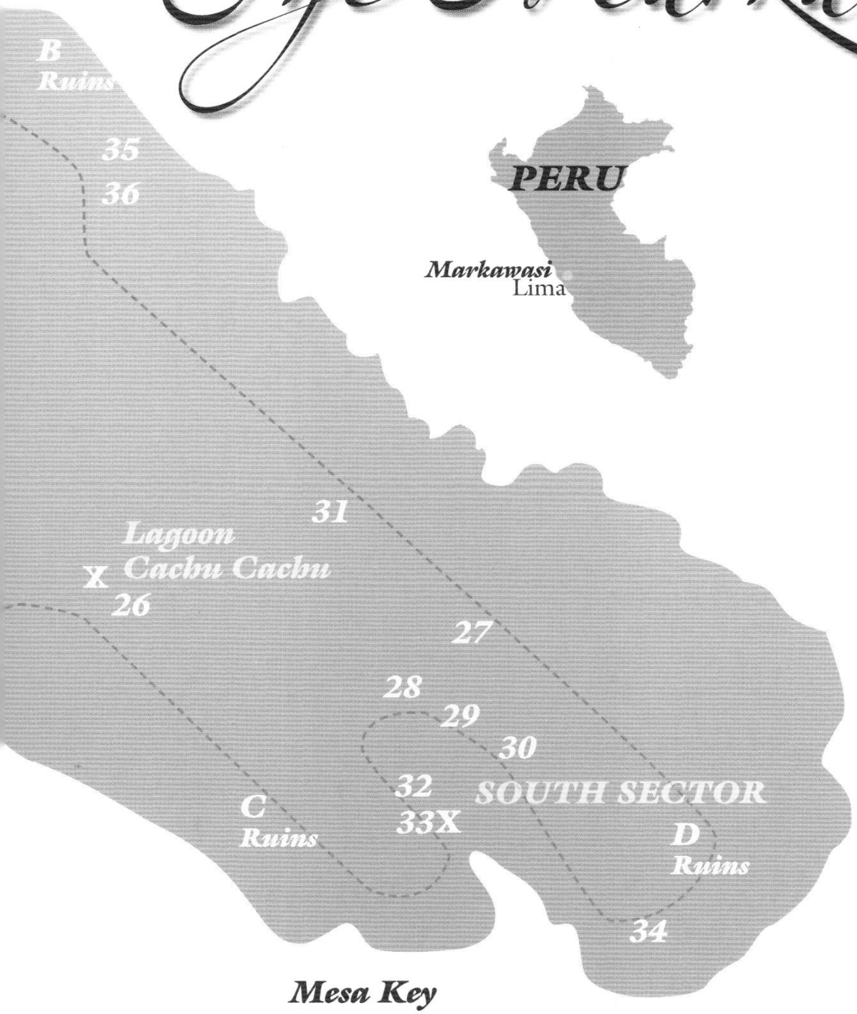

B Ruins

35
36

PERU

Markawasi
Lima

31

Lagoon
Cachu Cachu
X
26

27

28
29
30
32 **SOUTH SECTOR**
C 33X
Ruins

D Ruins

34

Mesa Key
Latitude S:11°46.309'
Longitude W: 76°34.724'
12,800' (above sea level)
Distance North to South: 2.8 Miles; 4.5 Kilometers

01 Monument to Humanity
02 African Lions
03 Turtle
04 Camel (two humps)
05 Woman with Child
06 Ruzo's Cabin, Elephant
07 Condors, Elephants
08 The Cave
09 Camel/Llama
10 Chullpas
11 Huacracocha Lagoon
12 Druid
13 Prophet
14 Pharaoh
15 Alchemist
16 Chinese Ideogram
17 Amphitheatre, Inca
18 The Lovers, Puma
19 Gate of the Gods
    Sphinxes, Mastodon, Bruja
20 Dogs, Frogs
21 Dancing Maidens Mayorales/Shell

22 Valley of the Sea lions
23 Pre-historic Tortoise
24 Inferno/Infernillo
25 Reclining Man
26 Fallen Horse, Cross
27 Egyptian Deities, Astronauts
28 Condor
29 The King
30 The Sphinx
31 Hill of Gazes
32 African Queen
33 Fortress, White Queen
34 Archaeological Remains
35 Santa Maria
    (highest point)
36 The Cat
37 Kankausho Altar
38 Seat of Soxtacuri

Vortexes are marked with an X

46

Temples of Light and Shadow

Monument to Humanity

48

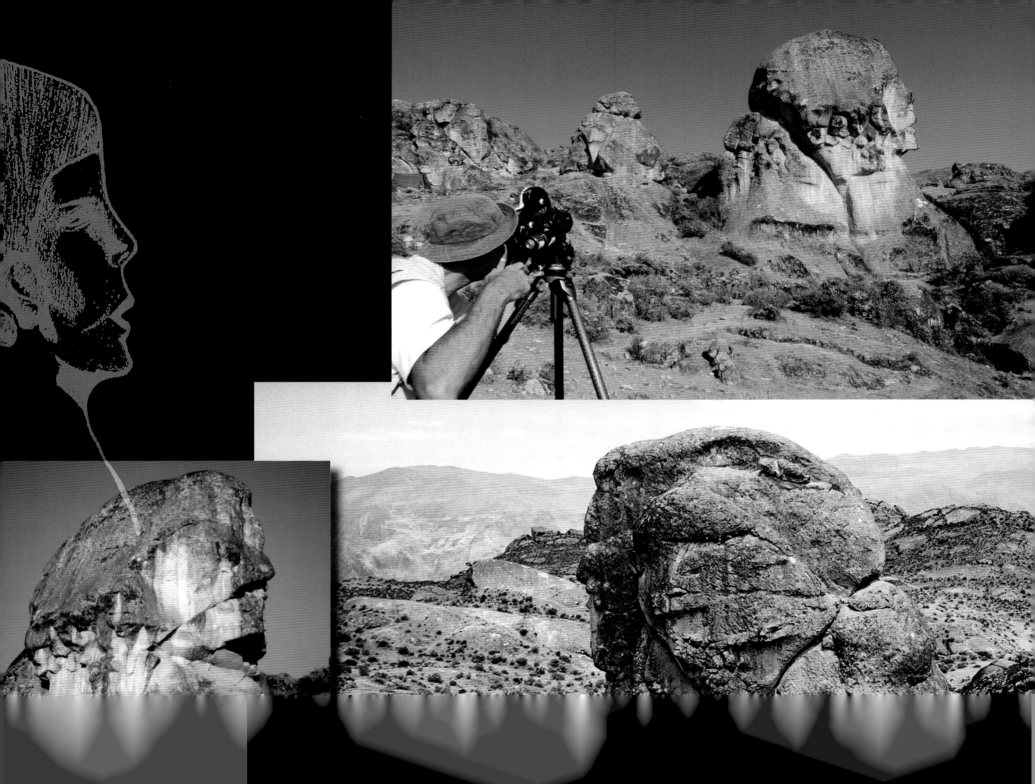

Monument to Humanity

"On approaching the top of the plateau we suddenly faced the rock of this story, seventy-five feet high on the western side and sixty on the eastern face. It can be considered a monument to humanity, erected in ancient times, since many sculpted heads of different racial characteristics can be discerned on it. The sculptors worked on the natural rock so long ago that no memory of them or of their creation's name remained. The old men of Casta say it was called 'Peca Gasha,' the 'head in the alley,' referring to its location at the entrance to the top of the plateau. In recent times it has been called the 'Inca's Head,' a name that to them implies great antiquity, although it has no relationship to the Inca empire."

Peca Gasha

Special stones were considered "stones that speak" and "the dwelling places of the Divine," where the biblical Jacob rested his head, and embraced prophetic vision.

As "thunder" and "lightning stones," they are linked with the internal fire of initiation, "kundalini."

51

Chessboard

Monument to Humanity

"… a noteworthy inscription is visible on an almost perfectly vertical surface. The technique used to engrave it is unique; we have never seen such anywhere else; from any angle other than the correct one this surface appears dotted by a fortuitous handful of lead shot. The double lines enclose a space representing the sixteen central squares of the chessboard."

"A simple figure, expressing the chessboard pattern, or two-dimensional space (like our modern graphs do), and subject to proportion by the cross, repeated at equal intervals, is also the central symbol studied in *The Signs* of Pedro Astete. The two figures that represent the chessboard are pentacles that evoke all the symbols that meet in chess. Astete had discovered that all the monuments found in Egypt have their counterparts in chess, the remains of forty centuries of their history. The pyramids are rooks; the sphinxes, horses and the obelisks are represented by the bishops; the colossi are the king and queen; the pawns that are reborn at the end of their journey stand for the Phoenix that is reborn from the ashes; the chessboard is the labyrinth, the structure found often under palaces and temples in Egypt. There are no other monuments there, if we consider all the possible representatives of the colossi." – Daniel Ruzo

Zodiac

"The other sign, the sun and its twelve rays, represents the eclipse and the twelve zodiac constellations. With those two very simple figures we have the evidence that the vanished people knew the symbolic system of chess and of the zodiac, inseparable parts of a total symbolic system that encompasses, in harmonious form, all human knowledge. A lithograph in black repeats this chessboard on the neck of the same sculpture, with the addition of two small black circles on a brown background with a central black dot. Perhaps brown was the original color of the figure. One of the circles is on the extreme left of the second row of squares counting from the top; the other is at the extreme right of the third row."

–Daniel Ruzo

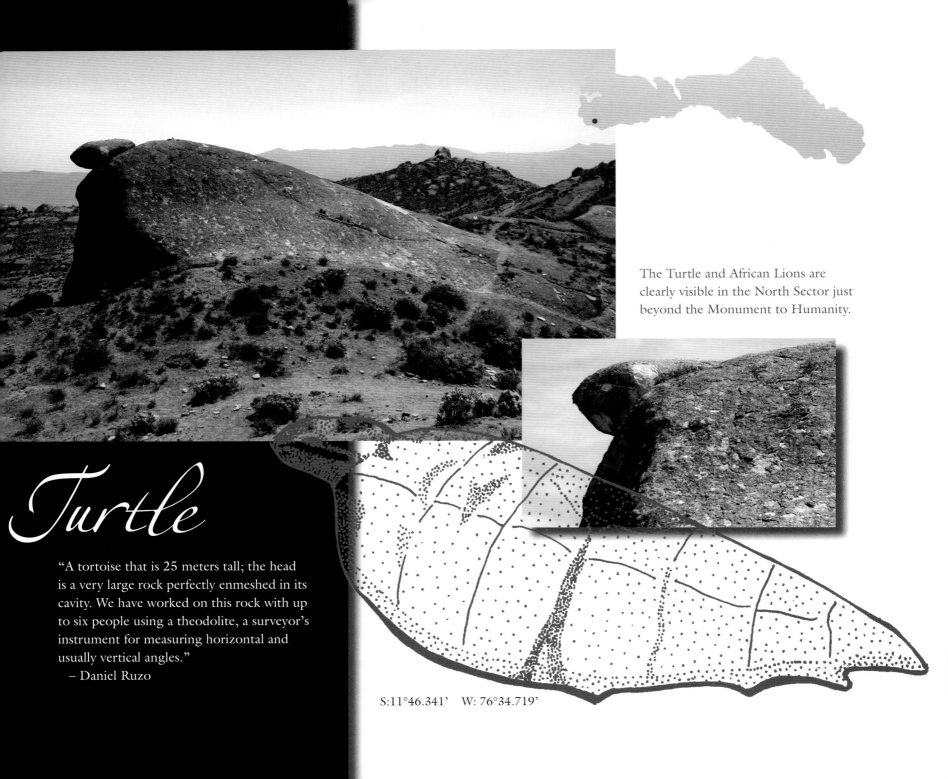

The Turtle and African Lions are clearly visible in the North Sector just beyond the Monument to Humanity.

Turtle

"A tortoise that is 25 meters tall; the head is a very large rock perfectly enmeshed in its cavity. We have worked on this rock with up to six people using a theodolite, a surveyor's instrument for measuring horizontal and usually vertical angles."
– Daniel Ruzo

S:11°46.341'   W: 76°34.719'

African Lions

Woman with Child

S:11°46.328'   W: 76°34.701'

A view of "Woman with Child," alongside the
Monument to Humanity.

We find a woman, pregnant with child, carrying another child wrapped in a traditional "manta," on her back. Andean families are typically large, with older children helping in the fields when not attending school, compulsory to the age of fourteen. The woman with child sits directly behind the Monument to Humanity, in the North Sector, and is easily visible.

Camp

S:11°46.356'   W: 76°34.711'

"We studied the Markawasi plateau for nine years. We constructed a hut and passed all the time in it that we had available during the dry months, from April to September. Only once did we climb in December. We verified, in those rare moments of sun, that some sculptures were made to be appreciated under the illumination of that solstice, which, at Peru's latitude, is the summer. In the Andes it is the period of great rains. After twenty days living within the humidity of a cloud cover that would not permit either vision or photography, we saw that we had to abandon our work. However, in the dry months the resplendent sun, in an absolutely clear sky, permitted us thousands of magnificent photographs." – Daniel Ruzo

In the 1950's, Daniel Ruzo built this small, single-room stone cabin for his base. Today, the cabin is still used, sometimes as a cook house, or for accommodation. Although it makes for meager shelter (it is drafty, with a dirt floor and metal roof), its proximity to key monuments in the North Sector couldn't be better. A more commodious alternative is to set up camp nearby in the horseshoe grotto, which is protected from the wind by soaring boulders on three sides, and is only a short walk to the cabin.

Druid

"Why this affirmation of the dolmenic religion upon the statue
that perpetuated the memory of an exceptional man if he was not a
druid? The meetings of the druids were secret. Today we have to say
'shamanic,' countering the dictionary. The humanities will follow
one another upon the earth until one distant day all men belong
to that dolmenic religion, based on the 'direct knowledge' or 'vital
knowledge' of the four elements, that did not, does not, nor will ever
have either rites or dogmas."
  – Daniel Ruzo

S:11°46.598'   W: 76°34.735'

The Pharaoh & Nefertiti

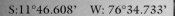

S:11°46.608'   W: 76°34.733'

The Pharaoh, with false, straight beard, wears the ruler's ceremonial "Nemes." Ruzo referred to this figure as "a personage of Egyptian dress, the image of a pharaoh before the flood," and theorized that the Egyptian images found on the mesa arose from an earlier proto-historical epoch whose traces may be found carved in stone on the Markawasi plateau.

The Pharaoh is found in the North Sector, along Sunset Ridge; the location of Nefertiti has become lost and is unknown.

Chinese Ideogram

S:11°46.746'   W: 76°34.585'

The language of the Chinese Ideogram remains a mystery; it has never been adequately interpreted. The Chinese Ideogram is best viewed in the afternoon sunlight when various effects are cast upon the rock. It is located along Sunset Ridge in the North Sector looking south to the Fortress.

Traversing the North Sector is photographer, Sean Adair.

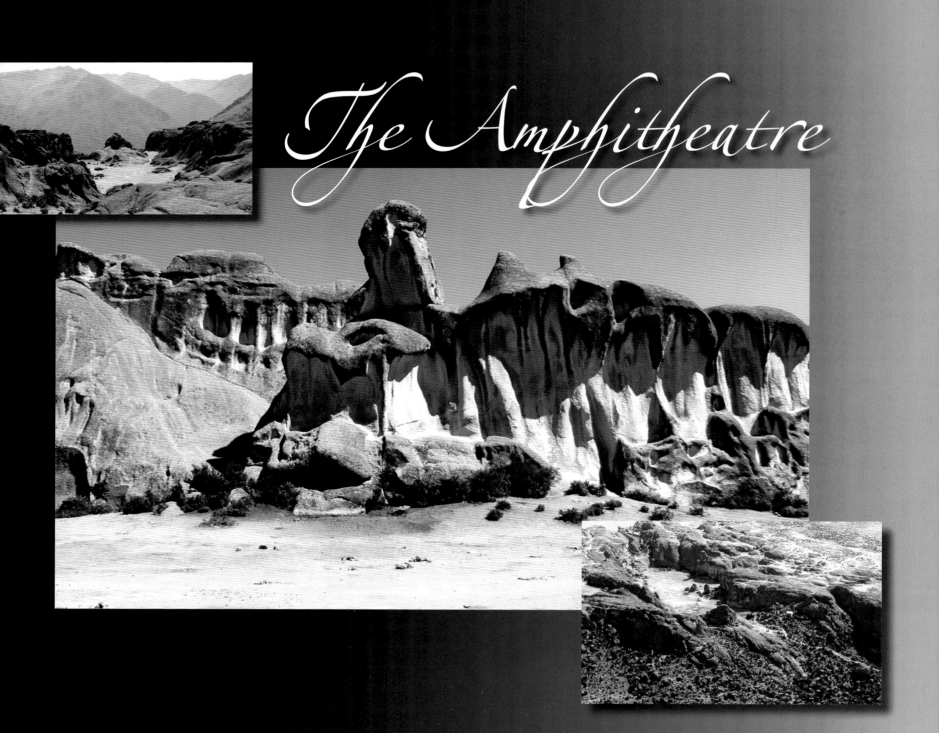

The Amphitheatre

Inca

The profile of an Inca gazes across the sprawling area known as the Amphitheatre; he wears a traditional woven head covering with earflaps: the conical-shaped "chullo." With soaring granite towers forming a natural alcove, whose shadows, some say, form the images of dancing maidens under the light of the moon, the Amphitheatre is a favorite site for campers. It is located near the center of the mesa in a natural hollow aligned east to west, Central Sector.

S:11°46.675'   W: 76°34.500'

The Lovers

A couple locked in an embrace. The man (left), with back turned away, embraces the woman who gazes forward. The Lovers, Puma and Seat of Soxtacuri are located in the eastern tract of the mesa near the Amphitheatre.

S:11°46.424'   W: 76°34.506'

Seat of Soxtacuri

Puma

"Soxtacuri was the living god who ruled over the entire plateau of Markawasi. Every year the people who lived in Markawasi would offer a sacrifice to their beloved Soxtacuri. One year the people failed to make their offering, and in anger, he left and moved to Bolivia. It is said that when Soxtacuri left, his godless people also moved from the plateau. By the time the conquistadores arrived, new peoples populated the meseta of Markawasi. Soxtacuri's house and seat (throne) still remain on the plateau."

— Lisa Rome

S:11°46.457'   W: 76°34.237'

Gate of the Gods

S:11°46.943'   W: 76°34.504'

Near the center point of Sunset Ridge we find the "Gate of the Gods," a conflux
of anthropomorphic and zoomorphic figures, including the Winged Sphinx, Frogs,
Great Toad, Dogs, Mastodon and the Bruja.

Gate of the Gods

Mastodon

In the region of Peru's Moche Valley, mastodons were killed by hunters using large tanged Paiján points. Growing to 10 feet in height and weighing up to 7 tons, mastodons, along with the woolly mammoth, became extinct around 10,000 BC.

The Bruja, Mastodon, Winged Sphinx and Great Toad (a sphinx, not shown) are located at the Gate of the Gods, in the Central Sector, near Sunset Ridge.

Bruja   *Mastodon*   *Sphinx*

Back view of
Winged Sphinx.

The Dogs

"On the mesa there are numerous zoomorphic vestiges. Besides the guardian dogs of the Treasure, that represent the dog Cerberus, there are fertile and symbolic animals. All express the fertility of the earth."
– Daniel Ruzo

S:11°46.972'   W: 76°34.454'

Frogs

(Great Toad)

As one circles behind the Great Toad, it changes into a sphinx, and then a frog, resembling other "frogs" located at the Gate of the Gods.

S:11°46.895'   W: 76°34.502'

Mayorales
The Shell

Dominating the Central Sector directly south of the Gate of the Gods, the altar of the Mayorales is a natural acoustic shell, where maidens would dance during the fiesta of Huari.

S:11°46.954'   W: 76°34.500'

The Dancing Maidens

Valley of the Sea Lions

"For that 'salvation' and for that 'rebirth,' humanity needs a 'matrix.' Surrounding the cave of stone we always find the symbol of fertility: the pregnant female hippopotamus, which is the Egyptian symbol of fertility; the nursing sea lioness, which is the fertility symbol along the coasts of Brazil; the turtles, symbols of fertility in Fountainbleau and Peru, where we also find the goddess Ta-urt."
– Daniel Ruzo

S:11°46.926'   W: 76°34.525'

Tortoise
(Anfichelidia)

"Pre-historic tortoise, the Anfichelidia ancestor of the tortoise, dates from the Jurassic period. The shell is divided into four parts. A moderately large tortoise, around four feet in length, the head, the tail and the limbs could not pull back into the shell, but were naturally protected by their contexture."
– Daniel Ruzo

Valley of the Sea Lions and the Tortoise are found in the Central Sector, south of the Mayorales.

S:11°47.145'   W: 76°34.402'

The Inferno
Infernillo

"The Inferno is a large rock crevasse, about twenty feet deep. It is said that anyone who dares to jump across the Inferno will be 'swallowed up' and taken inside the earth, never to return again. Another myth surrounding the Inferno is that if a person walks into the base of the crevasse, he will be taken inside the earth, go through the mountain, and come out at the mouth of a river far away. The person would never be the same again and unable to reenter society. He would shy away from humans as wild animals do. The locals do regard these as myths and readily jump over the gap of the Inferno."

– Lisa Rome

S:11°47.202'   W: 76°34.493'

Reclining Man

The reclining figure found on the Markawasi plateau gazes skyward in
quiet repose; he is reminiscent of another sky watcher: The Face on Mars.

S:11°47.236'   W: 76°34.472'

Condor

S:11°47.517' W: 76°34.495'

The majestic bird is seen in profile; as one walks around the monument in a counter-clockwise manner, the Condor appears to age into a mature adult. The monument prominently sits in the South Sector.

Fallen Horse

"The most ancient science of humanity has always been symbolized by the horse. Through their association, the horse and the horseman have symbolized the Cabala and the wise Cabalist. Finding this symbol at Markawasi, twice, makes us feel secure that it was a center of human wisdom that can be positioned in a time before the flood." – Daniel Ruzo

The horse is seen lying on the ground, his head tilted to the left; atop the horse, midpoint, can be seen another rock, forming the head of a rider, only visible from a certain point of view. The horse is located near Cachu Cachu lagoon.

S:11°47.398'   W: 76°34.394'

Ta-urt and Sobek

The Egyptian Ta-urt, followed by the crocodile, stands erect upon her rear hooves with human arms, a long wig, and round beret on her head. She is the pregnant female hippopotamus, the Egyptian symbol of fertility, a protectress against Typhonic powers, carrying an ankh and fighting the forces of evil. As "Mistress of the Horizon" she is identified with the constellation of the hippopotamus in the tomb of Seti I. Ruzo believed she was sculptured five times on the plateau, symbolic of the many proto-historical deities found on the plateau.

S:11°47.471'   W: 76°34.361'

Astronauts

Two uniformed men wearing identical "escafandra" deep-sea suits, or possibly space suits. Ruzo found similar images in Tepoztlan, Mexico on the bearer of the chest of the Treasure of Tepozteco. The two astronauts stand adjacent to Ta-urt on the South Sector, near the Fortress.

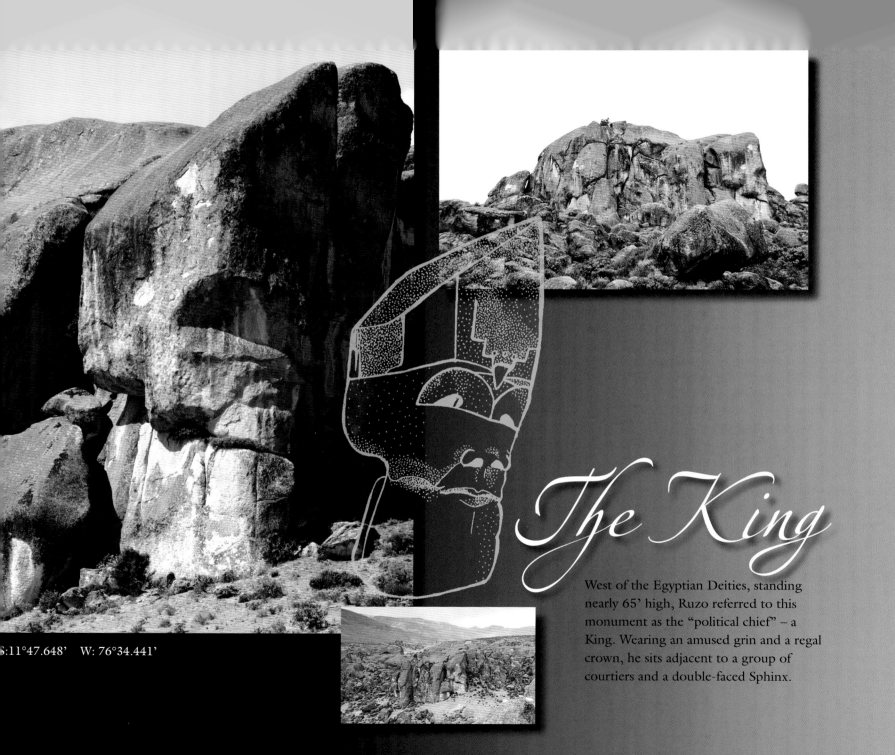

S:11°47.648'   W: 76°34.441'

The King

West of the Egyptian Deities, standing nearly 65' high, Ruzo referred to this monument as the "political chief" – a King. Wearing an amused grin and a regal crown, he sits adjacent to a group of courtiers and a double-faced Sphinx.

Sphinx

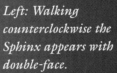

Left: Walking counterclockwise the Sphinx appears with double-face.

Cherubim are sphinx-like creatures guarding the treasure and sacred tombs; the "double-faced sphinx" sees with many eyes, and can be found in the South Sector along the processional path to the great Temple of the Ray, La Fortaleza.

S:11°46.895   W: 76°34.502'

There are twenty-two energy vortexes called cruzes or crosses, made up of three distinct types of energy. Three are found in areas of limited access on the plateau, for those prepared to be near

S:11°47.240' W: 76°34.384'

such powerful energy; seven crosses are betoken to the days of the week; twelve crosses have to do with the phases of the moon and each cross has a specific healing power.

The crosses, which are easily visible on the plateau, have an undeniable energy that can be felt without any special preparation, or sensitivity, as shown by Bill Cote (above), at Cachu Cachu Lagoon.

Cross / Cruz
Energy Vortexes

Above: Peter Schneider dowses the cross at Cachu Cachu Lagoon for magnetic anomaly.

Left: Robert Schoch checks for compass anomalies.

Hill of Gazes

One of the gazing figures.

S:11°47.671'
W: 76°34.466'

African Queen

The "Black Egyptian Goddess," as Ruzo called her, the African Queen gazes across the landscape from the rocky outcrop of the Fortress, considered a magnetic site.

  "I see it! She has her hair pulled back. Her profile looks like the profile of the Great Sphinx in Egypt; our forensic expert identified it as an African. When I saw the face at Markawasi, it reminded me of my old friend, the profile of the Great Sphinx. Now, is there a real connection here? Could there be some kind of connection between Peru, and ancient Egypt? I would say it's very weak evidence in and of itself in isolation, but put together with other evidence we have for inter-continental connections in ancient times, this seems to be just one more piece of the puzzle."

  – Robert Schoch   S:11°47.611'   W: 76°34.467'

The Great Sphinx of Egypt.

La Fortaleza

Continuing south from The King, legend says that at this point is found the treasure, referring to an "interior knowledge." The 130' outcrop is replete with Incan structures, dozens of figures and faces, including those of two queens: the White Queen (opposite page) and the African Queen, not shown. It is a well-known area for viewing OVNI's, as seen in photo, above right.

S:11°47.682'   W: 76°34.483'

The Fortress

A tall white rock pillar, shown prominently in the center of the Fortress, was deemed "The White Queen," by Daniel Ruzo.

Santa Maria

Located in the east south-central portion of the mesa, Santa Maria marks the highest point of the plateau, and has a seat carved into it from where one may view the cat at midday.

S:11°47.192'   W: 76°34.097'

The Cat

"On the most elevated tip of Markawasi's mesa and beneath the tallest rock that represents a venerable old man, carved into the natural stone is a perfectly identifiable seat. Always at midday, between the hours of twelve and one, we have seen the sculptured representation of a cat so perfectly that the shadow that forms its visible eye receives in its center a point of light that completes the image. The particularity of this sculpture is that it represents the cat with a closed mouth and with the tongue protruding. In Mexico, we found an Olmec piece with equal representation, as well as in the Louvre, where there are two Hittite pieces. In the museum at Athens, among the most ancient pieces whose age can not be determined, there is also a figure of Apollo that shows the tongue protruding, in spite of the mouth being closed."

– Daniel Ruzo

109

S:11°47.199'   W: 76°34.100'

Mask of a jaguar belonging to the Olmec culture.

Kankausho Altar

According to legend, the voice of the mythical character, Soxtacuri, remained in this altar. In the center of the altar is formed an acoustic shell, and a large rock in the image of a face with one eye; the other side of the rock is formed by a series of parallel chiseled lines, forming a line of reference with the highest point on the mesa, Santa Maria.

Kankausho is located along the eastern-most tract of the mesa; a perfect spot to behold the sunrise.

S:11°46.660'   W: 76°34.254'

Superbatolite Circompacifique

Dr. Robert M. Schoch, Ph.D.

The rock that composes the Markawasi Plateau is predominantly, and somewhat monotonously, a light-colored (gray to white in most regions, weathering to various tans, browns, and grays) diorite of the diorite-andesite family. In some cases the rock grades into what may be referred to as a granodiorite.

Ruzo (1956) states that the rock of Markawasi corresponds to the "Superbatolite Circompacifique" (Circumpacific Superbatholith), the mass of which is composed of "granodiorita" (granodiorite). The diorite of the plateau is in some cases, but not always, porphyritic. Essentially the diorite of Markawasi is similar to common granite except that it is relatively lacking in quartz and potassium feldspar; rather the diorite is composed of predominantly sodium-calcium plagioclase feldspars and ferromagnesian minerals. Among the pre-Columbian ruins on the plateau are blocks of red aphanitic andesite.

All of these rocks are igneous. The diorite is an intrusive rock that cooled from magma well below the surface of the Earth, while the andesite is an extrusive (volcanic) rock that cooled and solidified at the surface of the Earth. The rock now exposed at Markawasi is part of a huge batholith, one of many batholiths in the Andes. These batholiths are the result of the subduction and melting of lithosphere where two tectonic plates converged. The smashing together and crumpling of the plates caused earthquakes and igneous activity, and formed the Andes Mountains. Melted rock (magma) rose and formed batholiths. Subsequently the rocks above a batholith may be weathered and eroded away, mountain building continues, and the rocks of the batholith are exposed at the surface. It is interesting to note that the name andesite is derived from the Andes Mountains where rocks of the diorite-andesite family are so commonly found. Based solely on my field observations, I could not determine how old the diorites and andesites of Markawasi are; in order to firmly date these rocks various forms of radiometric dating might be applied. However, from a geologic point of view, the Andes are a fairly young mountain chain, having formed

within the last hundred million years or so (compared to over four billion years of Earth history). Indeed, the Andes continue to grow due to the tectonic activity of the region.

The Markawasi Plateau, like much of the Andes, was subjected to glacial conditions during the last ice age, which peaked perhaps 22,000 years ago and came to an end within the last 10,000 years. Much of the gross geomorphology of the region that we observe today may have been shaped during this period.

Once exposed at the surface, diorite (which originally formed under intense pressure deep below) is unstable and starts to weather and exfoliate. The minerals break down on the surface of the rock; cracks and weak zones are enhanced as water enters, freezes, and ice expands, further widening cracks. Changes in temperature throughout the course of the day, and throughout the year, stress the rock, and it slowly breaks down. Organisms, such as lichens, attach to the rock surfaces, eating away at the mineral content, causing further weathering and erosion. Wind and rain scour the rock surfaces and carry away particulate matter, which continues to move downhill under gravity. All of these processes result in

the formation of rounded, anthropomorphic and zoomorphic forms in the rocks as the weathered surfaces continue to expand and the weathering front also penetrates deeper into the rock itself. In some cases it is quite conceivable that natural zoomorphic and anthropomorphic forms may have been "helped along" by people who recognized the images and statues in the rock and judiciously broke away pieces along natural weak zones (where the rock would have eventually broken away of its own accord) to enhance the process of forming recognizable monuments. I could not find any definitive evidence of chiseling or other artificial working of the rock to form the monumental stone sculptures, but if such evidence ever existed, it may be long gone due to the natural weathering and erosion of the stone surfaces. Certainly humans have been visiting and carrying out activities on Markawasi for a very long time, as attested by the various ruins, waterworks, and graves found on the plateau. Whether or not they helped create the stone monuments of Markawasi, I am certain they recognized them as clearly, or even more clearly, as we do today.

113

Faces & Sculptures

simulacra

Sons of the Ray

by Marino Orlando Sanchez Macedo, Ph.D.

13th – 16th Century
Hydraulic Metropolis

To climb to the sacred mountain of Markwasi is a true magical and religious pilgrimage, because at the end of the sacred road lies the giant unfinished pyramid of this Andean Olympus, at whose top is the threshold of the celestial Gods—the shining hierophants, chief priests of the Eleusinian mysteries, or more appropriately, the Sons of the Ray, Thunder and Lightening, the pre-Hispanic God of the Mountains of the Northern Andes. In traditional literature the "shining ones" are always related with that which is unusual, singular, new, perfect or monstrous, becoming vessels of the magical forces, and, depending on the circumstances, revered or feared by the yearning of souls. In this central region of Peru the principal elements of worship are the Gods who control the annual seasons, bringing the waters, and subsequently the divinities of fertility.

To step on the top of this pyramid is to satisfy secret longings, to join and breathe in divine space, to prove through the senses the existence of natural divinity full of rocky images, distributed like a celestial crown. Rational logic is challenged by way of historical footprints in one of the most difficult geographic areas on earth. A rich pharmacopoeia of medicinal plants, the bounty of the mesa, provided the ancient healers remedy for physical and spiritual ailments. The man of Markawasi succeeded in dominating his inner being with technological knowledge, art and spirituality, in compliance with the gods and goddesses, for the purpose of managing the earth, the water, and time itself.

117

An Earthly Paradise

Entering the mesa through any one of the six entrances is akin to arriving to an earthly paradise wherein soft morning breezes envelope like a sleep-induced cocoon, inviting one to supper with the celestial Gods. A tenuous drizzle welcomes the visitor with sparkling rays, sifting through the invisible realm, cleansing the soul. During the rainy months (December through March) one enters on carpets of flowers. This is the spiritual scene where the ancient Markawasi chose to build a hydraulic metropolis—the kingdom of the Sons of the Ray near the celestial Gods, from where the water emerges hidden within the earth.

From the mountain the landscape diminishes into the distance, calling attention to the abysses and plummeting stairways, shrouded in mist. On clear nights, the stars descend so close that one could nearly touch them. From the West, brilliant rays reflect off the sea. There are other atmospheric phenomena of which there is no explanation. Certainly they present themselves at any moment with elongated, circular or oval form, and sometimes emanate strong lights that blind the eyes.

Incredibly, it is the animals that are the ones who sense the phenomena first. When a blinding ray falls close, the burros know beforehand. If they are tied up near a rocky crag, they push into it as if glued, and the ones not tied up hide themselves where they can. Only the wise know how to read nature, the University of Life teaches us daily.

In October the rains begin, becoming more profuse during the following months. The countryside is covered in green flowering plants. When the change of seasons occur the cold increases, and the fields are covered with solitary cacti and barren rock. The winter's fog prevents one from seeing the constant presence of fox, zorrinos, lizards, vizcachas; there are ducks and birds within the lagoons, and with luck one might sight the majestic flight of the solitary Condor, gliding through the open sky, serving as backdrop to the mythic battles between the coastal God Wallallo Karwincho and the God of the Mountains, Pariacaca.

The archaeological footprints of the ancient Markawasi speak of a fortified hydraulic metropolis with urban centers, defended both physically and esoterically, each having palaces, courts, houses, corrals and cemeteries, where the dead were ceremonially interred.

A Gigantic Crown on Top of the Mountain

The enigmatic forms sculpted by the rocks have created a series of conjectures, theories, and hypotheses that possess an esoteric, metaphysical, and parapsychological construct. Ultimately they speak of a psychic conception and even of an extraterrestrial origin. The esoteric may be found in the sphere of occult and magical knowledge, and therefore in the hands of certain individuals or adepts. As far as their origin, the proof must be found on the mesa itself, the visibility of which is not as clear as one would like. For the geographer the stone forests are simply part of the geographic fabric of the place, while for the historian, archaeologist, and anthropologist, they represent a natural landscape.

This immense rock display played a defensive role in pre-Hispanic antiquity, making Markawasi a fortified metropolis with a tie to the spiritual, gifted with a supernatural force, the "apu" (sacred guardians) who serve as the spiritual caretakers of the metropolis. The fabulous landscape inserted itself into the consciousness of the ancient people who considered it the abode of spirits, genies, and the God of the Waters.

He went on to say that they only viewed two additional spheres the following night, and then had wondered where all the objects had gone.

Maybe they had another appointment?

Although my story is, at times, difficult to fathom, it has been truthfully and accurately recorded, and I remain hopeful and encouraged. I see this as a time for a rebirthing of our paradigm; one that is based on the principals of a holistic worldview of peace, compassion, and service for the highest good— the ideals of the sacred feminine/masculine.

As each of us cross a threshold of awareness, a seeding takes place to discover our own innate wisdom. If we are mindful, we will discover new worlds, and new ways of expanding our wildest dreams. What we dare to dream is only limited by our imagination, that part of us that is infinite: an affirmation that we are not alone.

Kathy Doore

"E.T.", staring back at me. Laughing, I reached for the journal and opened it to a headline that read, "Fourteen UFOs Sighted Above Trout Lake, WA." I knew instantly that these were the same luminous spheres we had seen at Markawasi that night. The sighting had occurred during the exact time period that we were on the mesa, several thousand miles away.

According to the periodical's editor, "The objects appeared as small, luminous spheres flying back and forth across the sky in the upper atmosphere, approximately two to three times the brightness of the brightest stars. They flew at varying speeds, flaring and dimming as they went, and sometimes changed directions, all without making a sound. One anomalous light was a brief, intense flash, roughly four to five times brighter than the brightest stars."

Acknowledgements

During the production of this book, I was in touch with many people on three different continents, thanks, in great part, to the wonders of the internet. I would like to express my sincerest gratitude to the many individuals who gave their encouragement, support, and insight throughout the creation of this book.

My deepest, heartfelt thanks go to Peter Schneider, for his intense passion and encouragement in underwriting the project. Peter and I had long spoken of producing a book together, and it is due to his perseverance that we were ultimately able to give birth to the story, and bring it to a much greater audience.

I would like to pay special tribute to Dr. Robert Schoch, for his literary genius and depth of insight for generously introducing this work, in addition to providing a geological summary.

I'd like to thank my editor extraordinaire, Rea Day Baker, for her daily dose of wit and wisdom; had it not been for her tenacity, keen eye for grammar, and meticulous sense of detail in translation, this book would not have seen the light of day. I also direct my appreciation to Pat Alles, for her technical vision in artistically conveying the beauty of the mesa to the printed page.

Special thanks to Lydia Colon, who created the intuitive drawings shown throughout the guidebook, sketched from atop her mountain villa, Quilla Villa, in the Sacred Valley of the Incas, Peru. The many photos featured throughout the guidebook are the combined effort of several individuals. I would specifically like to thank photographer, Sean Adair, for use of his stunning images, and Bill Cote, for creatively bringing the Stone Forest to life through the visual medium. To my dear friends, Peggy Stok and Lydia Ruyle, who traveled with me to Markawasi, my deepest thanks for your generous contributions. And to Aanjelae Rhoads de Montero and her husband Lucho Montero, for their kindness, assistance, and exquisite photography of the healing plants found on the mesa, my deepest thanks.

To Dr. Marino Sanchez, particular thanks for his scholarly essay on the archaeological remains; and to Lisa Rome, for her exceptional historical retrospective of Daniel Ruzo's work, and her account of the medicinal plants found on the mesa.

I'd like to express profound gratitude to Pablo Chong, for generously sharing his personal story, and to his wife, Mignon, for her assistance. I was surprised to learn that Pablo had received confirmation of his experience in much the same way as I had, via the synchronicity of a periodical, the same method of validation that confirmed "The Dream of Masma" to Pedro Astete--the dream

170

that started it all! Erik Mendoza first shared his personal tale with me in the late 1990's, while arranging my group tour to Nazca. Erik, without doubt, is the most skilled guide on the mesa (providing the GPS coordinates for this book), and sees to all the practical details with dedication. I highly recommend his services to anyone contemplating a journey.

My appreciation goes to my dear friend, Annette Everitt, who journeyed with me to the Stone Forest in 2001 and shared her story; the first of many such adventures we would make together and the "stuff of which dreams are made". To my dear, intuitive friend, Stephanie Phelps, a debt of gratitude for her extraordinary communiqué, transmitted with grace and great care. Thank you.

I'd like to extend the most heartfelt gratitude to the entire Ruzo family: to Daniel Ruzo's widow, Carola Cisneros de Ruzo, who hosted me in her home in Lima, where the idea for this guidebook first arose, and who graciously permitted excerpts from Daniel's archive along with personal photos; to Daniel's son, Daniel Ruzo, a great scholar and visionary, for his encouragement and support; and to his son, Javier Ruzo, a gifted poet and painter, who contributed an essay to this book and archival footage.

My deepest appreciation, love and gratitude, go to my friends and family for their support of my work, and lending a sympathetic ear when I needed one.

I extend my appreciation to the people of San Pedro de Casta, guardians of the meseta, for their continual dedication, care, and protection of the ancient Stone Forest. And, last, but most assuredly not least, to the Apu of Markawasi, the Spirits of the Mountain, my gratitude for the

Carola Cisneros de Ruzo

gentle reminder: we are not now, nor have we ever been, alone, in our extraordinary journey of remembrance, *our Divine heritage*.

Kathy Doore
Phoenix, Arizona

171

Contributors

Over 400 Color Photographs, Illustrations & Maps

Credits Key

r=right; l=left; c=center; cl=center left; cr=center right; tr = top right; tl =top left; bl=bottom left; br=bottom right; bc=bottom center

Featured Photographers

Adair, Sean: pages 2-4, 7, 14, 16-18, 29, 31, 32, 40-43, 46, 47, 49 tr, 50 r, 53 r, 54 cl, 55 tl, 56, 57 tr, 58 tr, 58 bl, 60, 62 l, 63, 65, 67, 69 rt, 69 bl, 73 bc, 73 br, 74 bl,78, 79 r, 80-82, 83 bl, 84 r, 85, 88 tl, 90 to, 91, 92, 95 bl, 96 l, 97 tl, 99, 102, 104, 106 tr tl, 109 br, 110, 112, 114 tr tl, 115 tr tc bcr,116, 117, 118 tr,121, 123 bl, 126, 130, 131, 132, 133 tr, bl, 134, 135 tl, 136, 138, 139, 140 cr,142-145, 158 bl, 160 tl, back cover tr br

Schneider, Peter E.: pg. 4 tr, 5, 6, 8, 10 br, 12 br,13, 15, 19, 20, 22, 23, 34, 48, 52 tl, 52 br, 53 tl, 53 cl, 54 tl, 55, 57 c, 61, 62 r, 64, 66, 68, 69 tl, 73 l, 74 bl,75 c,76, 79 tr, 80 br, 84 l, 86, 87, 88 bl, 89 br, 89 bl, 90 tl, br, 93, 94, 95 tc, 96 c, 97 tr, 98, 99 bl,100, 101 l, 103, 104 bl,105,106 bc,107 bl, 108, 109 tl, 111, 113, 114 tc br bc, 115 cr br, 118 bl, 119, 120, 124, 126 b, 127-129, 135 cl, bl, 137 tl, 155, 161 tr, back cover tl

We gratefully acknowledge the written contributions of Robert Schoch, Lisa Rome, Javier Ruzo, Marino Sanchez, Lydia Colon, Pablo Chong, Annette Everitt, Erik Mendoza, Stephanie Phelps, Peter E. Schneider, and the excerpted works of the late Daniel Ruzo and Pedro Astete.

Contributing Photographers

Aliaga, Maria Eugenia: pg. 118 bl

Alles, Pat: pg. 148, 149

Chong, Pablo: pg.155

Colon, Lydia: pg. 152, 153, 154

Cote, Bill: pg. 29 bc, 52 tr

Doore, Kathy: dedication page 1, 5, 9 bl and tl, 10, 24-27, 28, 33, 38 bc, 50 tl, 58 top left, 59 cl, 70-72, 75 r, 135 r, 148, 157, 159, 164, 166 tr, 167, 168, 169, 171, 172

Downey, Edie: pg. 165 left center

Einsiedler, Manfred: cover, pg. 161 r

Everitt, Annette: pg. 133 br, 163

Phelps, Stephanie: pg.160

Rhoads de Montero, Aanjelae: pg. 9 tr, 10 tl, t, 12 tl, 83 c tr, 94 tl, 122, 146, 147, 172

Rome, Lisa: pg. 140 bl, 141, 147

Ruyle, Lydia: pg. 167 bl

Ruzo, Javier: pg. 30, 35-37, 38 tr, 39, 59

Sanchez, Marino: pg. 51, 65 tl, 77, 89 tc, 101 r, 107 tr

Schoch, Robert M.: pg. 105 br

Stok, Peggy: pg. 158 tr, 166 bl

Artists

Colon, Lydia: pg. 44, 47, 48, 49, 54, 55, 57, 60, 61, 64, 74, 75, 76, 81, 82, 83, 87, 88, 89, 92, 93, 95, 96, 97, 98, 99, 100, 101, 105, 109

Doore, Kathy: 27, 28, 45, 70, 71, 78, 79, 91tl, 103, 123, 125, 132, 176

For more information on the Markawasi Stone Forest including featured treks, tours, updates, and people who have contributed to this book, please visit us online at

Markawasi.com

Suggested Reading etc.

Bradt, Hilary. *Peru and Bolivia: Backpacking and Trekking*. The Globe Pequot Press, 1974.

Campbell, Joseph. *The Hero with a Thousand Faces*. Bollingen; Reprint edition, March 1, 1972.

Cayce, Edgar. *Edgar Cayce on Atlantis*. Warner Books, 1988.

Churchward, James. *The Lost Continent of Mu*. New York: William Edwin Rudge, 1926.

Cobo, Father Bernabe. *Inca Religion and Customs*. Edited and Translated, Roland Hamilton. Austin, TX: University of Texas Press, 1990 (1653).

Cote, Bill. BC Video. *The Mysterious Stone Monuments of Markawasi Peru;* DVD. BC Video, New York, 2007. *The Mysterious Origins of Man,* Series; DVD; *The Mystery of the Sphinx*; DVD; www.bcvideo.com.

Ebeling, Klaus. *Marcahuasi: A Forgotten Site of Monumental Sculptures in the Peruvian Andes, Field Guide and Catalog*. 1984. 52 pages.

Garcilaso de la Vega, El Inca. *The Royal Commentaries of the Incas, 1539-1616*. Trans. Harold Livermore. Austin, TX: University of Texas Press, 1966.

Guenon, Rene. *Symbols of Sacred Science*. Sophia Perennis, New York; 2004.

Hall, Manly P. Hall. *The Secret Teachings of All Ages*. The Philosophical Research Society, 1945.

Hancock, Graham; and Faiia, Santha. *Heaven's Mirror: Quest for the Lost Civilization*. New York: Random House, 1998.

Hapgood, Charles. *Maps of the Ancient Sea Kings: Evidence of Advanced Civilization in the Ice Age*. Kempton, Illinois: Adventures Unlimited Press, 1997.

Henry, William. *Starwalkers and the Dimension of the Blessed*. Scala Dei; 2006.

Heyerdahl, Thor. *The Art of Easter Island*. New York: Doubleday, 1975.

Hurtak, J.J. *The Keys of Enoch: The Book of Knowledge*. Academy for Future Science, 1977.

Jenkins, John Major. *Maya Cosmogenesis 2012*. Bear & Company, Rochester, VT. 1998.

Joseph, Frank. *The Lost Civilization of Lemuria: The Rise and Fall of the World's Oldest Culture*. Bear & Company, Rochester, Vermont. 2006.

Kaku, Michio. *Hyperspace: A Scientific Odyssey Through Parallel Universes, Time Warps, and the 10th Dimension*. New York: Oxford University Press, 1994.

Mack, John E. *Passport to the Cosmos: Human Transformation and Alien Encounters*. New York: Crown Publishers, 1999.

Michell, John. *Confessions of a Radical Traditionalist*. (Essays by John Michell, Selected and Introduced by Joscelyn Godwin). Waterbury Center, Vermont: Dominion, 2005.
Simulacra: Faces and Figures in Nature. Thames and Hudson, 1979.

Ponce De Leon Paiva, Anton. *The Wisdom of the Ancient One: An Inca Initiation*. Amber Lotus, May 1995. *In Search of the Wise One: A Sacred Journey*. Bluestar Communications 1996.

Pauwels, Louis and Jacques Bergier. *The Morning of the Magicians*. London: Souvenir Press, 1960.

Paz, Sixto Wells. *The Invitation*. Fairfield, IA: First World Library.

Roads, Michael J. *Talking With Nature: Sharing the Energies and Spirit of Trees, Plants, Birds, and Earth*. H.J. Kramer, 1987.

Routledge, Katherine. *The Mystery of Easter Island*. Kempton, IL: Adventures Unlimited Press, 1919.

Ruyle, Lydia. *Goddess Icons: Spirit Banners of the Divine Feminine.* WovenWord Press, 2002.

Ruzo, Daniel.
El Testamento Auténtico de Nostradamus. Barcelona: Plaza & Janes, 1975. *Los Ultimos Dias Del Apocalipsis.* Cuernavaca, 1990.
El Valle Sagrado de Tepoztlan: Los Temples Atlantes de México. Lima: Editorial Mundo Hispano S.R.L., 1978 (fourth edition).
La Cultura Masma. L'Ethnographie. Revue de la Société d'Ethnographie de Paris, 1956.
Marcahuasi: La Historia fantástica de un Descubrimiento. Lima: Ignacio Trapero, 1974;
Le plus ancien "haut-lieu" du monde? Planète, no. 3. Paris, February-March 1962.
Preliminary Investigations of an Unknown American Race. Communication made before the National Academy of Sciences of Mexico on January 19, 1953.

Sanchez, Mario. *De Las Sacerdotisas, Brujas y Adivinas de Machu Picchu* (The Priests, Witches and Soothsayers of Machu Picchu). Cusco, Peru: Empresa Editora Contental Peru S.A., 1989.

Santillana, Giorgio de; and von Dechend, Hertha. *Hamlet's Mill.* David R. Godine Publisher; 1992.

Sarmiento, Pedro de Gamboa; (1532-1608). *History of the Incas.* Toronto: General Publishing Company, 1999.

Schoch, Robert M.,
with Robert Aquinas McNally. *Voyages of the Pyramid Builders: The True Origins of the Pyramids, from Lost Egypt to Ancient America.* New York: Penguin Putnam, 2003.
Voices of the Rocks: A Scientist Looks at Catastrophes and Ancient Civilizations. New York: Harmony Books, 1999.
Pyramid Quest: Secrets of the Great Pyramid and the Dawn of Civilization. New York: Penguin, 2005; www.robertschoch.net.

Sheldrake, Rupert. *A New Science of Life: The Hypothesis of Formative Causation.* Los Angeles: J. P. Tarcher, 1981.

Simpson, Liz. *The Magic of Labyrinths* : *Following your Path, Finding Your Center.* Thorsons, 2002.

Sitchen, Zecharia. *The Lost Realms: Book IV of the Earth Chronicles.* New York: Avon Books, 1990.

Spence, Lewis. *The History of Atlantis.* New York: Bell Publishing, 1926. *Evidence of Atlantis from Old Peru.* Kessinger Publishing, December 2005.

Sullivan, William. *The Secret of the Incas: Myth, Astronomy, and the War Against Time.* Three Rivers Press, 2003.

Talbot, Michael. *The Holographic Universe.* Harper Perennial, 1992.

Taylor Hansen, L. *He Walked the Americas.* Amherst, WI: Legend Press, 1963.

Villoldo, Alberto. *Island of the Sun: Mastering the Inca Medicine Wheel.* Destiny Books, 1994.

Weidner, Jay; and Bridges, Vincent. *Monument to the End of Time: Alchemy, Fulcanelli and the Great Cross at Hendaye.* Destiny Books, 2003.

Wilcox, Joan Parisi. *Keepers of the Ancient Knowledge: The Mystical World of the Q'ero Indians of Peru.* Boston: Element Books, 1999.

Wilkins, Harold T. *Mysteries of Ancient South America.* New York: The Citadel Press, 1956.

Williamson, George Hunt. *Road in the Sky.* London: Neville Spearman, 1959 (third impression, 1969). Brother Philip (pseudonym of George Hunt Williamson). *Secret of the Andes.* London: Neville Spearman, 1961 *Other Tongues—Other Flesh.* Amherst Press. 1953.
Secret Places of the Lion: Alien Influences on Earth's Destiny. Destiny Book, 1996.

Tell me a story
About a magic moon
That lights a crystal kingdom
On a purple shore,
Not too far from now.

Fill that land with wonders
With people, not like us,
Who do impossible
Deeds in places we've
Never been, nor will be.

New creatures that have
Names hard to say
And do improbable
Feats with power and grace;
And are forever, free.

Let's draw a map
That points the route
To this fabulous world,
So close, so near.
Then take my hand
And lead the way.

Hanna